Voyage

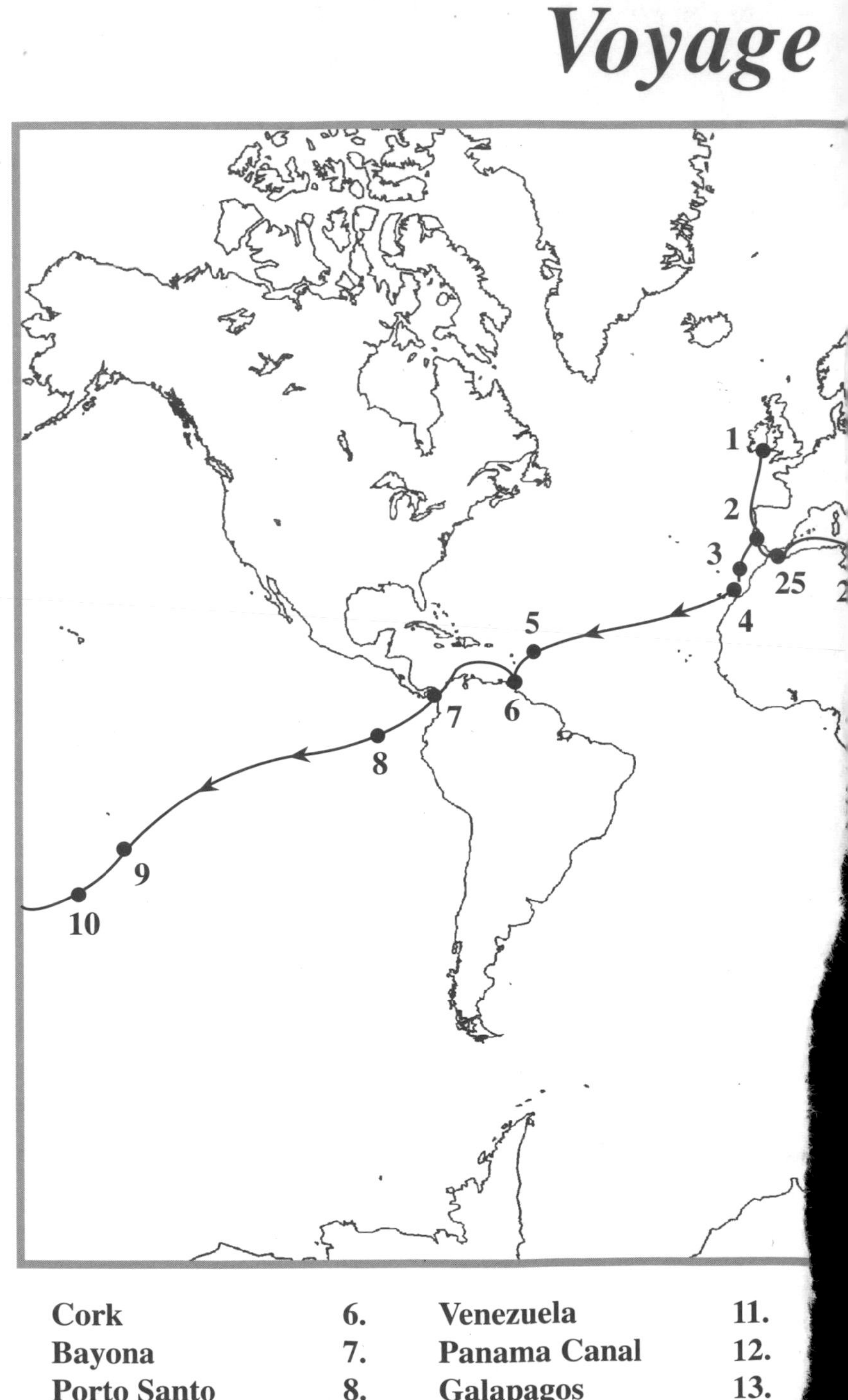

1. Cork
2. Bayona
3. Porto Santo
4. Canary Islands
5. St. Lucia
6. Venezuela
7. Panama Canal
8. Galapagos
9. Marquesas Islands
10. Tahiti
11.
12.
13.
14.
15.

Of Hope

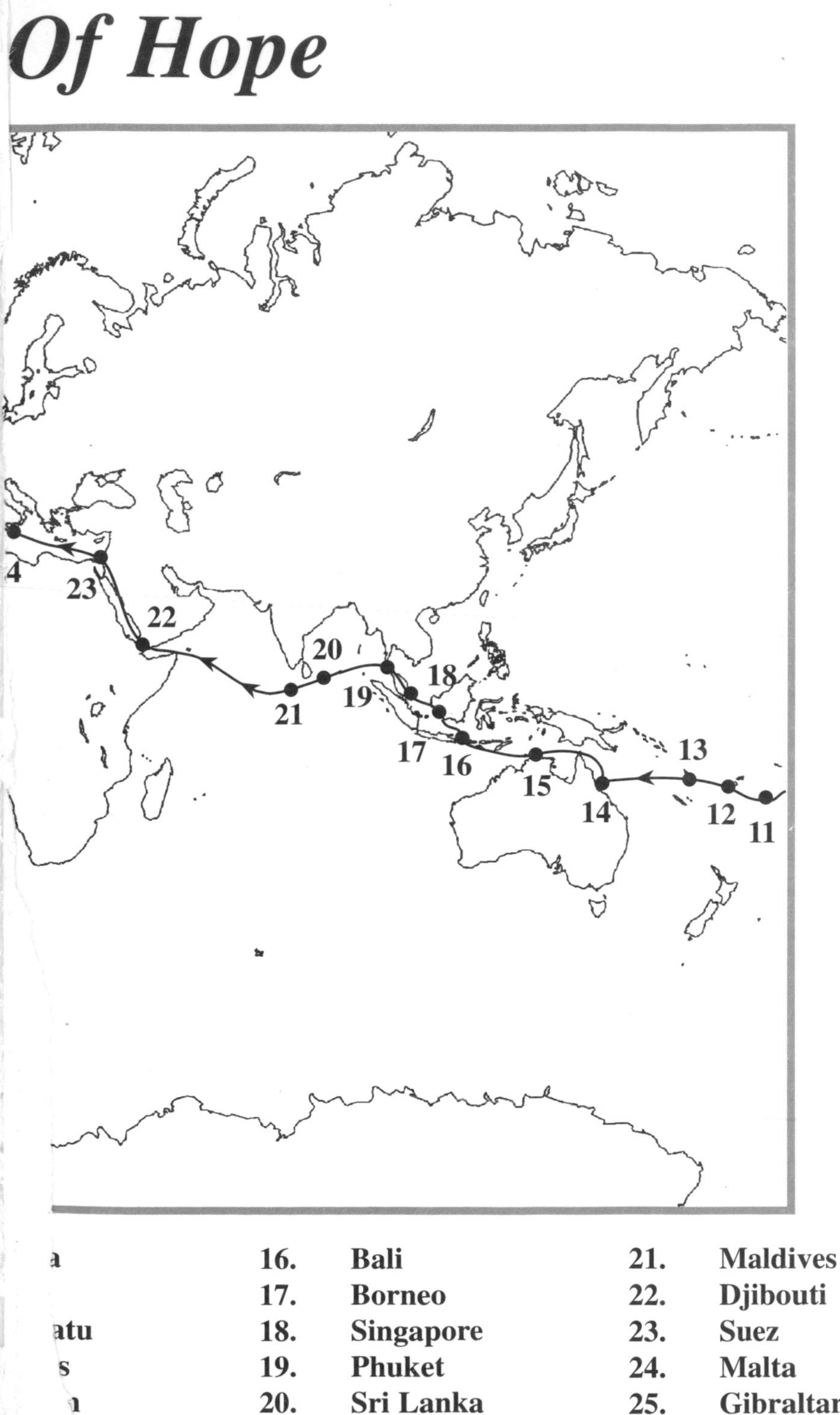

a	16.	Bali	21.	Maldives
	17.	Borneo	22.	Djibouti
atu	18.	Singapore	23.	Suez
s	19.	Phuket	24.	Malta
n	20.	Sri Lanka	25.	Gibraltar

Voyage of Hope

Sail Chernobyl

Rory Coveney

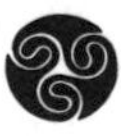

Mercier Press

MERCIER PRESS
5 French Church Street, Cork
16 Hume Street, Dublin 2

Trade enquiries to CMD DISTRIBUTION,
55a Spruce Avenue, Stillorgan Industrial Park, Blackrock, Dublin

ISBN 1 85635 221 8

10 9 8 7 6 5 4 3 2 1

TO MUM AND DAD
FOR EVERYTHING

Printed in Ireland by Colour Books Ltd.

CONTENTS

Acknowledgments

There are many people I would like to thank for their help both in the writing of this book and for their support for the duration of the Sail Chernobyl Project. There are three people I would like to especially thank for their unwavering support and commitment to my family and this project. Terry Prone of Carr Communications, was one of the first people we went to with this whole idea and her enthusiasm and advice from the early planning stages through to the publication of this book has been wonderful – we are all very grateful. Likewise Mimi Doran, the project co-ordinator, worked tirelessly to make this project a success. Thirdly Adi Roche whose commitment to what she is doing proved an inspiration to all of us. Without these three people Sail Chernobyl could never have happened the way it did.

From the very beginning the Carr Communications team of Dave Curtain and Gemma Nally, and James O'Sullivan and Mike Brady of Aardvark Internet Publishing were tremendous. Keeping our story alive for nearly two years was a vital and very difficult task and without these people we could not have achieved anything like the profile and subsequent support from others that we did. They were as important as we were in trying to raise money. Allied Irish Bank and Murphy's Irish Stout were our main sponsors and we are very thankful for their belief in us and the financial support they gave the project from the beginning.

We are very grateful for the support of the Irish government and in particular An Taoiseach Bertie Ahern who opened the project in October of 1997, Minister for Education Micheál Martin and the Department of Foreign Affairs.

There were many companies who contributed to Sail

Chernobyl and I would like to thank them very much: KPMG, Barlo Plastics, Ford, Aer Lingus, Mercier Press, Carrigaline Court Hotel, *Irish Times*, Royal Cork Yacht Club, University College Cork Sailing Club, Dublin Port, ScoilNET.

Likewise there were some people who made a fantastic contribution and I would like to thank them: Tish and Noel Canniffe, Tom Kavanagh, Mr & Mrs Roy Disney, the people of Tracton parish, Noel Smith, Jim Hennessy, Michelle O'Connell, Pat Lake and all at Castlepoint Boatyard, Noel Noonan, John Dempsey, Brian Smullen, Donal McClement, Kevin Lane, Dick Gibson and all the members of the Royal Cork Yacht Club, Clayton and Betty Love, Liam Coughlan, Mary Lynch, Bernie Cahill, Frank and Barbara Fitzgibbon, Tony Cassar, the Two Daves and Edwina from Malta, Fr Bert, Eric, the crew who delivered *Golden Apple* to Tahiti; Jeano, Ted, Giles and Al, Oliver and Kate Harte, Paddy Cantillon, Andrew and Shelby Brown, SuperGran, Christy Moore, Olive O'Sullivan, Janice and Gwen from F.22, Denis MacSweeney, Peter Barry, Gary Horgan, Dave Kiely, Paddy Munden and the crew of *Passiona,* Fr Conor Harper, Barclay Clibborn, Colm O'Sullivan, Nellie, Irish Marine Emergency Services, the Irish Navy, in particular the captain and crew of the *Aisling*.

The media were very good to us throughout this whole project and we very much appreciated their help. In particular I would like to thank the following people: Lorna Siggins, Anita Whooley, Jim Gallagher, John Green, Neil Prendeville, Derek Davis, Tom McSweeney, Pat Kenny, Rockin Jerry, Mark Kelleher and John Sheehan.

The schools in Ireland were wonderful throughout our time away, their support and interest gave us a great sense of belief in what we were trying to achieve and I would like to thank the children and teachers and I hope they enjoyed the story. I would like to thank one school in particular. Clongowes

Wood College did a fantastic fundraising job and I would like to thank Frank Kelly, Brian O'Keeffe, Pat Linane, Fr Bruce Bradley and the students for their great effort and support.

Numerous friends of ours helped in a variety of ways and we very much appreciated their help. My good friends were people I missed very much over the past two years and I would like to thank the following for their constant support in terms of letters, emails and phonecalls and also for their advice in putting together this book: Kielo, Fitzy, Whip, Mark and the Australia crew, Rose, Dom, Aido, Maura, Heffo, Andy, and Thea.

I would like to thank John Sheehan and *The Examiner* for the use of their photographs; and Michael B. Yeats for permission to quote from W. B. Yeats' 'The Song of Wandering Aengus'.

Lastly I would like to thank my family, both the crew and the others, who have been fantastic throughout the last two years and have put up with me while I put this book together. I could never have done it without their support, criticism and advice.

FOREWORD

Christy Moore

I have been eagerly awaiting the publication of this book. There are many things about this heroic voyage that have intrigued me.

We crowded around the North Wall of Dublin Docks as the Voyage of Hope was about to begin. There was a wonderful atmosphere amongst the crowd that included An Taoiseach, politicians, clergy lads, business honchos great and small, publicists, journalists, photographers, latchicoes, crowd control engineers, and a good few of us who had no real jobs at all. At the nub of the gathering stood the Coveney family side by side with the people of the Chernobyl Children's Project.

What struck me most that morning was the mixed expressions of pride and concern upon the faces of Hugh and Pauline Coveney as they watched five of their seven children preparing to set sail to God only knows where.

The sailors brought me on board and gave me a grand tour of their vessel. To this claustrophobic landlubber the conditions were very cramped and I reckoned that living at such close quarters for eighteen months would severely test any family, I'd have been overboard before The Pigeon House at the end of the Liffey. For me, while aboard, it was nice to see a few of my albums in the music rack.

Off they sailed and we heard occasional reports of their progress. I faxed them a few short notes once or twice and thought little else of their whereabouts until the dreadful news of Hugh's tragic death resounded around the country. Our minds were filled with thoughts of their little craft upon the vast ocean and the terrible news that awaited them. Having suffered a similar loss, as a young boy, I am deeply curious to understand how they managed to cope with this unique situation.

It has been a privilege to write these few words, to be involved in some small way with the Voyage of Hope. I wish the Coveney family long life and happiness and I trust that the Chernobyl Children's fund will benefit greatly from their heroic efforts.

1

BEGINNINGS

How could I possibly have expected it to turn out the way it did? It's hard to know where to start when trying to cover the last two years of my life, so much has happened and changed, that at times I have to pinch myself to actually believe it has all been real. It is difficult to know where to start but I suppose I should start with the people I was to spend nearly two years with, namely my brothers and sister.

Simon is a farmer. Or at least he was a farmer before we left; of course he is now a TD, so I had better be careful what I say about him. He had been working for the Crowleys, for the year before we left, on their farm in Mallow as a trainee manager learning the intricacies of the land and cultivation. By the time we were ready to leave, his hands were worn from piking bales and his upper body tanned in that T-shirt sort of way from the summer harvest. Simon was always an adventurous type. In February 1997 he climbed Mount Kilamanjarro in Africa, he courageously vomited his way to the summit, ill with altitude sickness, determined not to fail. He has a history of stupid driving and almost more than anything loves marmalade on soft doughy bread. He speaks well in public, dances with a shoulder shuffle and much to my despair likes Garth Brooks. He is in fact rather more sophisticated than I have portrayed him so far, and certainly has become so since Dad died. He was to begin the journey as skipper.

Andrew does the type of engineering that involves diodes, transistors and things that most of us find utterly confusing. Andrew is shy, determined, wears glasses and has, much like me, a badly receding hairline. He is the most experienced sailor of all of us having started competitive dinghy sailing at the age of seven. He does things rather than talk about them, he hates lists and study plans and just gets on with it. He also, despite his engineering training, tends to smear jam or honey on his cheeks as he eats a slice of toast. He, oddly, combines incredible aptitude for things technical with utter clumsiness for things that are not. Andrew was to be the navigator and general fixer of things.

Tony spends an awful amount of time positioning his eyebrows, particularly for the camera. He is, although we hate to admit it, the best looking of the brothers, but despite his rather suave appearance is in fact, like his twin, quite shy and incredibly well mannered. He has a goofy walk although he does his best to cover it up with an over the top gait. Tony is one for strong opinions and when he gets into one of his preaching moods is more dogmatic than the Pope. Oddly however he does combine conservative dogmatism with a willingness to try anything once. He has incredible attention to detail but unlike his twin, Andrew, it is with the aesthetic rather than the technical. He is the kind of person who would spend hours polishing a three-legged table and not worry about whether it would stand. Tony was the cook, which is in line with his training to be a hotel manager. It was his responsibility to feed us around the world.

Rebecca qualifies everything she says with 'do you know what I mean', and invariably we don't. She was the youngest member of the crew and the only girl. Rebecca talks a lot. Before this trip she had never really been away from home and she had an endearing naiveté that was rare among nineteen-year-old girls. She is ferociously determined and like Tony can at times be both argumentative and stubborn. Rebecca like me is grumpy in the mornings and is at her worst before noon. She is a little clumsy, has a sweet tooth, and has a huge appetite for fun. She was to be the medic and radio operator.

Then there is me, Rory. Luckily considering I am writing this I don't have to give away too much about myself, at least not at this stage anyway. I suppose there is a piece of each of the others in me, I would like to be able to say that I am courageous like Simon, technical like Andrew, aesthetic like Tony and fun-loving like Rebecca, your all round balanced hero, but I am afraid I can't say that. In theory my character should come through the text – so who knows maybe you will be able to figure out what I am like by the end of this. The story of the next two years is, and can only be, my view of things. I don't pretend to know what the others were thinking and while I may speculate at times, for the most part, they will be my feelings on what is going on.

We had all been brought up with the sea. Over the years Dad had always been in and around the sea, from racing boats to fishing boats and this had rubbed off on all of us. The idea of sailing around the world was always a distant dream but one that none of us ever thought would happen. Like most things it began as a small idea.

Andrew wanted to take a break from his course in university. Engineering is demanding and, unlike the Arts degree I had done, was very much full time. Typical of Andrew in the two years he had completed he had got two first class honours despite not really enjoying it. He wanted to bring the boat across the Atlantic and maybe work in the Caribbean or America for a while. He first went to Simon with the idea around Christmas 1996. Simon was very enthusiastic, within a week we were all interested, and approached Dad as we were going to have to borrow his boat. We would certainly need his help and luckily he was very supportive from those early stages. Soon the idea was expanded to go the whole way around the world.

Planning to sail around the world is something that most

people take years to decide and organise; we had about six months from when we agreed that we all wanted to do it. After much consultation among ourselves and various experts we concluded that it was possible for us to do it in a minimum of eighteen to twenty months. This may seem like a long period but the important consideration was of course the weather. First of all we had to plan to avoid all the major hurricane and cyclone seasons in various parts of the world; namely the Caribbean, the South Pacific and the monsoon cyclone season in the Indian Ocean. Likewise we had to avoid times when there would be no wind, we only had a range of about 1,000 miles under engine, given the amount of fuel we could realistically carry, so we would need wind, particularly for the long stretches in the Pacific.

The other consideration was our various careers. Simon as I have already mentioned was a farmer, with the ambition of running our farm, so for him it was easy enough to put that on hold. Andrew, Tony and Rebecca were all in the middle of degree courses at university so for them it was more difficult to arrange time off. We were going to be away for two academic years. Both Tony and Rebecca's course directors were enthusiastic about the project and agreed to give the time off. Andrew's situation was a little more difficult considering the rapidly changing nature of the electronic engineering world, but in the end they agreed. For me the situation was more personal. Having completed a history degree, I had then already spent a year working and travelling in Australia before returning to Ireland to do a Diploma in Business Studies in Dublin. Before the idea of the trip had come up I was anxious to start a career. Initially I wasn't going to go, but Dad soon persuaded me, saying that it was a fantastic opportunity and would definitely, in his view, be beneficial for future employment.

We all agreed that we wanted to try and use what we

going to do to help a charitable organisation. It would be a unique family challenge and we believed it could, if managed and organised properly, be a good way of generating public interest. We decided to approach Adi Roche of the Chernobyl Children's Project to see if she might be interested.

You might ask why Chernobyl? Firstly we had always, like many people, admired the work that Adi Roche and her team do. But perhaps more importantly we wanted to help an organisation that was Irish but was at the same time addressing a global issue that would be relevant no matter where in the world we went. Many people have since asked me why we didn't try to help a home-based charity. My answer has always been that if you are trying to raise money and awareness for something uniquely Irish, no matter how worthy, it would be almost impossible in far-off places like Thailand or Australia. This may sound very calculated and before I went to Belarus I suppose it was. Adi Roche thought the idea had fantastic potential and was enthusiastic from the beginning. She was very anxious that at least one of us would come out with her to see for ourselves the problems that Chernobyl had caused. As the others were all working at the time I was the only member of the crew able to go.

◊

As the plane came through the clouds and I looked out the window everything appeared normal; I could not taste, feel, see or hear any danger. I suppose I didn't know really what to expect, maybe scorched earth, withered trees, two-headed cows, at least some visible signs, but no, everything appeared the same as in Ireland. It was a little unnerving knowing that the most lethal poison in the world was everywhere but invisible. It is in the air, water, food, the land itself, cloaked in the ordinary – slowly killing everything.

The plane was full of children returning from their stay in Ireland and once we made sure all the children were reunited with their families we headed to the first of the orphanages. It was here that I first started to see what Chernobyl had done. As I walked through the wards of this cold place many of the children were deformed and retarded. One particular child has since remained vividly in my memory. The child's head was horribly swollen, her face was perfect amid this awful deformity, her complexion was a deathly white, almost purple, her eyes were black, lifeless and full of tears, she was screaming but there was no sound. This I was told is the silent scream. It is an agony without a voice or sound, a slow crushing of the brain, heart and soul. This little girl had a hydrocephalic head and had not long to live.

We left Gomel the following morning and made our way by train to Minsk. As we passed through the countryside it was hard to believe that all I could see out of the windows was so dangerous. It must be so difficult for the native people I could see in the fields and towns to understand. The train travelled through the night and by early morning we arrived in Minsk.

On our second day we went to Radaskovichi, some twenty miles south of Minsk, a rural area where many of the people from the Chernobyl region are relocated. We visited a house where the grandmother, or Babuska as they are called here, told her story. This old woman is very proud and as she speaks she weeps but through these tears came a terrible anger.

'I used to live in Bragin only 45 miles from Chernobyl and now I can never go home, I can never see my friends again, I can never see my farm again, they have given me nothing in return, I wasn't allowed take anything and they told us nothing. We only knew there was something wrong when all the doctors started to leave. For months we lived there not knowing if anything was wrong, the children played outside and now most of them are sick.'

The Chernobyl Children's Project had that summer brought the children from this family to Ireland and they were due back in a few days. They were incredibly grateful for what Adi had done for their children and especially for listening to their problems. After we had spoken to the grandmother we were invited into the kitchen for food and drinks. The room was small and we all crowded around the small table. The mother gave us all they had, tomatoes, meat, bread and, of course, vodka. By the time we had each given a toast which is customary we were all a little drunk and for a while everything seemed all right as the people in the room joked and laughed.

Later as we were returning to Minsk I tried to imagine what it would be like if something like this happened in Ireland. I tried to picture my own grandmother and how she would feel or how I would feel if I could never go home again, if I could never again see any of my friends. It's hard to get any true understanding of what these people have endured and are still experiencing. Much later on when we were in Panama I met a woman from another boat and was telling her about my visit to Belarus and how difficult it was for me to imagine how the people must have felt. She said to me that unless you have experienced terrible loss and grief it is impossible to understand – she was right.

The Children's Cancer Hospital in Minsk is full of youngsters with thyroid cancer. One in four children in Belarus now develop thyroid cancer as a result of the Chernobyl accident compared to one in 1,000,000 in the rest of the world. Most of the children are quite young and don't really know what is wrong with them. Little Ena was only twelve when she talked to me about her dreams of being a famous painter – she did not seem to understand that she might never fulfil these dreams. A future here is so uncertain. Some have had the operation to remove the thyroid gland while many are waiting to have it – walking around with lines drawn across their necks where the incision will be made. This is called the Belarusian Necklace.

It was only when I returned to Ireland that I realised the magnitude of the problems Chernobyl has caused and how important the work of the Chernobyl Children's Project actually is. What had started for me, at least, as simply a worthy cause and something that was complementary to what we were trying to achieve, now took on a whole new meaning. I know it sounds trite to say that the visit to Belarus changed me, but it did. For someone as lucky and fortunate as I have been seeing and feeling something like this was entirely new and very humbling. It put into perspective what is important and what isn't. For me what differentiates Chernobyl from other disasters is the fact that it can never be properly fixed – famines and poverty while tragic are inherently fixable at least in the medium to long term. The people of Belarus will suffer from the effects of Chernobyl for generations, indeed, forever.

In this world there are people with good intentions and ideas and those who have neither. There are also people of action and courage and people who just talk. Fortunately for the people of Belarus, and indeed many others, Adi Roche is a woman who falls into the ideal category – a woman of that rare combination of both courage and goodness. There are many people who are cynical about the work of Adi and her team but they really have no idea what she is doing or how important her work is to these people. But as Theodore Roosevelt said 'it's not the critic who counts, nor the person who points out how the strong person stumbles or where the doer of deeds could have done better. The credit belongs to the person who is actually in the arena, whose face is marred by dust and sweat and blood; who knows of great enthusiasm, great devotion and the triumph of achievement – so that his or her place shall never be with those cold and timid souls who know neither victory nor defeat.'

Adi's arena is a tough one – the least we could do was try to help her to compete.

◊

From July until we left in October we all did our utmost to put the pieces of this project together. There were so many elements to try to get organised that sometimes I wonder how we were ever ready to leave for nearly two years.

We were very lucky to have a boat like *Golden Apple*. Most people see boats much as they view cars, for working or as a means of transportation. *Golden Apple* was for us very special; she was to be our means of travel and, more importantly, our home for nearly two years. *Golden Apple* had originally been built in Crosshaven in 1979 for a Norwegian who had ambitions to circumnavigate the world. Unfortunately he died before the boat was finished and never got to fulfil his dream. Dad found her in the south of England in the beginning of 1991 looking dishevelled and very uncared for but felt he had found a real gem. When she arrived back to Cork she had grass growing on the deck and all the varnish and paint-work was peeling and bleached. Over the next few years she was meticulously restored by her original builders. By the time we had decided to head around the world she was nearly ready to go.

We were confident the boat was capable of withstanding the constant pressures that such a voyage would place on it. There were, however, many things that had to be added and changed to add to the safety of the trip and improve our communications. Navigation equipment in the form of charts, books, guides took up a lot of space. We had to carry charts for the entire world, every port and every dangerous rock. Andy spent weeks at home in the dining-room trying to figure out the logistics because as navigator it was important that he knew where we would be going. Tony and Rebecca both did a course in First Aid and we had medical equipment for almost every type of emergency, from pain-killers to ice-packs to antibiotics. We were lucky to have the help of good friend of ours, David Kiely, a surgeon. Bec and Tony even practised stitching on pigs' trotters.

We turned the front cabin of the boat into a work-bench. We knew that no matter how well prepared we were we would definitely break things and need somewhere to fix them. We installed a vice and we had all sorts of tools from wrenches to hammers to drills. By the end of the trip we had all become good at fixing things and improvising with what we had to sort out what ever problem arose.

Some of the people who had originally built *Golden Apple* were of great help to us in preparing her for her greatest adventure. Most of them now were old and brought wisdom and experience to the total planning. They knew what we would have to face and they knew every inch of the boat. Before we left Pat Lake, the head foreman of the team who built her, told me that he had never built a stronger boat. These veterans were very proud of this boat and were all a little teary when they saw us head off.

There was the task of figuring how we were going to try to raise £1 million. Media interest was going to be essential if we were to raise anything close to that amount of money. Luckily Terry Prone of Carr Communications was captivated early on by the idea and once she met Adi she agreed to do all the PR for the trip. Sponsorship from the beginning was proving difficult to obtain. Simon and myself had been to a number of big companies and we didn't seem to be getting anywhere. We did manage to secure some sponsors, Murphy's Irish Stout agreed to host six fundraising events around the world. Allied

Irish Banks came on board, so to speak, in that they agreed to pay a project co-ordinator for the duration of the project. This person was to be responsible for all fundraising activities back home in Ireland and, where possible, help us plan and organise events along the route. After a few interviews Mimi Doran, a schoolteacher, was selected for the job. She was tremendously enthusiastic from the beginning, which was very important considering the length of the project. The other important element to put in place was our website as we decided this was the best way to keep the story alive for people while we were away at sea. The great thing about a website is that it has permanent air-time and we are able to change it and add to it to keep people interested. Aardvark Internet Publishing, a company based in Cork, were already hosting the Chernobyl Children's Project website and after a meeting with them they agreed to design and manage our site. Much later on the Sail Chernobyl website was to become the second most popular website in the country and vital in terms of raising money.

In early August we brought some children from the Chernobyl region out on the boat. Simon and Andrew were away in England at a seminar on world cruising, so Dad agreed to help out with Rebecca, Tony and I. The children were in Ireland as part of Paul Newman's Barrettstown camp – a holiday centre for terminally ill children from all over the world. Many of them had not seen the sea before and just gripped the railing looking out at the water not really understanding. I can clearly remember a little boy who quietly ate his way through four bananas in a row. He could not believe that he would be allowed to do so, as bananas in Belarus are very rare. Little Sasha, who has lost all his family, and most recently his brother, was terribly shy of the cameras and huddled up to Adi as if she were his mother. After we came back in there was a party for the children in the yacht club and as a way of saying thank you they sang a Russian song. It was a very sad sounding song, but then again, for me at least, most things Russian conjure up images of things sad, particularly their music. But it was a sad moment and everyone in the room seemed to feel it, many people cried, as these little children, who were so sick, sang their hearts out.

One of the funnier moments of the day was when Dad crashed the boat as we came in. There was a look of complete despair on his face and thinking about this still makes me smile. It was not very often that my father made a fool of himself, well publicly at least.

By the start of October most things were in place and we were ready to launch the project. While we hadn't raised that much money a good system was in place that we hoped would, over the course of the nineteen month voyage, generate considerable funds. We were all a little nervous at how the media would react to the whole idea. I think Dad was particularly worried that it might be perceived as a cynical method of improving his own political profile. But the launch in Dublin turned out to be a great success and was a political mix by virtue of the people who were there. An Taoiseach Bertie Ahern of Fianna Fáil officially launched the project. I'm not sure how comfortable he was on the boat mind you, he was very shaky as the boat rocked and we had to hold him as he hoisted the Sail Chernobyl flag. Adi Roche who was then standing in the presidential election for the Labour Party was also there, and of course Dad was there, who as you probably know was at the time on the Fine Gael front bench. There were also some celebrities, which always helps, in the form of Ali Hewson and Christy Moore. Typically my mother didn't know what Christy looked like and was a little shocked to see this big guy in sandals and a T-shirt climbing onto the boat talking to Rebecca. It was a great boost to get this type of support and made the countless cheesy photographs, that Dave Curtin from Carr and

Mimi were getting us to pose for, a little easier to stomach. A big crowd from the media turned up and we were absolutely delighted with the coverage the next day in the press, and that day on the various radio channels. The following week was a hectic one of last minute details and lots of interviews. In the end it was a relief to leave on 17 October. Each of us was as ready as we were ever going to be.

2

The Horizon Circled Us

The sea was rough and glistened with a blinding reflection. It had been a wet Irish summer and the land still had a green shine even in the autumn sun. Below the stove rocked on its gimble, see-sawing, betraying the irregular pattern of the cold water all around us. We were glad it was sunny, it made the departure a little easier, and a gloomy sky would have exaggerated the worried look on our dear mother's face. That week had been a tough one for her. I suppose it was only natural that she was anxious, the thought of losing five of the children she had laboured so hard to produce was a little much for her. Both our parents seemed proud, and that made us happy. Being the son or daughter of a proud parent is a warm feeling. We finally left Cork not really knowing what to expect but looking forward to it all the same. Behind, the white-haired wake made a v-shape to the stern and the coast slowly disappeared into the sky. Our home had shrunk into fifty feet of wood, a shared space where we would all live for the next year and a half. Gone were our friends, girlfriends, boyfriend and family. I don't think any of us had really thought too much about what we were leaving behind, and if it would be there when we returned. We had been so busy getting everything ready for this day that we didn't have much time to think about anything else. We all thought about it then and for just that moment we were, each of us, a little lonely.

The waves parted in front of us and the wind pushed us quickly as night fell. The wind blew from the north-east, cold but not too strong. The moon was high in the sky and its face danced, broken on the waves. Tony went down to the galley and adapting well to the now moving cooker, prepared a dinner of bangers and mash. We were all hungry and ate furiously from the metal dog dishes that Mum had given us. The rim of the dishes held the rolling sausages in, while the mash wobbled. For the first time we all began to feel tired. The euphoria of our departure began to wane and the reality of a long sea passage began to sink in. Throughout the night there had to be someone up on look-out, usually we had two. The watch system rotated with each person doing his or her allocated slot. On this first night as the weather seemed settled we decide to go for the one-person watches. My watch would begin at twelve and would go on until two. I tried to get some sleep before then.

It's a little unnerving being the only one awake out in the middle of the ocean. All around is a vast moving darkness. Not being able to see accentuated my other senses, particularly my hearing. All was dark but for the small radar screen and the light from the moon. Everything was quiet but for the sound of the water and the odd creak from the rigging. After a while my eyes started to adjust to the dim light and as I looked up I could see the sails silhouetted against the moon. My mind wandered back to the previous weeks and the day that has just passed. My crying mother, dying children, photographers everywhere. What a few weeks it had been. Leaving a loved one at the train station, excitement about the trip, tremendous excitement – the ultimate adventure, the enchantment of the sea, an odyssey. I was going on a real odyssey – the South Seas, the Caribbean and the South China Sea, all before us. So much depended on this whole project, not least thousands of children in Belarus, as we were the main fundraisers for the Chernobyl Children's Project that year. I remembered the day we brought the children out on the boat and the endless preparations – from impact screwdrivers to Internet sites and everything in between. Thank God we are gone at last. The clouds covered the moon and it was time for me to go to bed. I woke Tony for his watch.

The morning sun arrived and with it came the dolphins. They effortlessly swam with the boat, playing with the bow wave and each other. The sun was on their backs, and they shone silvery only a few inches under the surface. Every ten seconds or so they jumped, with such ease their whole bodies flipped out of the water. We all got the feeling they were enjoying our admiration and were showing off their grace. They stayed with us for about fifteen minutes and then they were gone as quickly as they had come.

It's amazing how quickly we all settled into our roles on the boat. Andrew, within twenty-four hours of us leaving, was down in the engine room battling with the electrics. Things are always breaking on boats. The trailing generator had broken already. He was covered in tools and wires and his glasses fogged up from the heat of the engine. Tony started the cooking early that day; determined to show us he was capable of producing something a little more flamboyant than his dinner the night before. Simon was overseeing everything, it's incredible how much he enjoyed just sailing the boat, he didn't need any other stimulation. I was trying desperately to understand the Immarsat C system – a communications system via satellite – that enabled us to receive and send email messages to and from anyone, using the laptop computer. It also gave us most of our weather information. The barometer had been slowly dropping, a bad sign and we were anxious to get a weather forecast. Meanwhile Rebecca was steering.

I finally managed to figure out the computer and the forecast was bad for the Bay of Biscay. The weather station in Toulouse was predicting a force seven to eight with big swells and we were heading into the tail end of hurricane 'Grace', wind strength was going to increase to storm levels and seas to match. None of us had been out in weather like that before and certainly not this far from land. We all knew we would encounter severe weather at some stage in the trip but I don't think any of us believed it would come as soon as twenty-four hours after our departure. We knew we were in for a long night.

The first gust hit when Andrew and Tony were on watch. We were all awake, our senses sharp to the ever-changing elements. Lying in my bunk I could feel every wave, the boat was slamming hard into the seas – the sound was almost deafening. Suddenly the intensity of everything increased and the roar of the wind escalated to a high pitch. Simon and I jumped out of our bunks to see what was happening. We couldn't see Tony who was steering the boat from the aft steering wheel. Hailstones were falling in sheets.

'I think we are in the middle of it,' Andrew shouted to Tony, from the radar monitor as the squall formed a massive blob on the screen.

'No shit Andy,' Tony yelled from behind the waterfall, shielding his face with his arm, crouched behind the wheel post.

There were nervous laughs as the boat heeled once again and the water lashed the glass on the doghouse windows that protected us. Tony reappeared from the black wet night, smiling and soaked. The oilskins made him look huge, the hood covered his head, the rest of him covered with red and white canvas. Boots on his feet. His face was bare like an open window to the storm. Simon and I in contrast were in our boxer shorts shielded in the cabin, thanking God we were not out there. Our watch would come. The gust calmed again. The rest of the night was spent trying to avoid the squalls using the radar. We tried to sleep while off watch but we were not yet used to the strange sounds. I thought of those who were fast asleep tucked in their beds and wondered what the hell I was doing.

The following morning we could see the waves that had been shaking us through the night. They didn't appear as menacing as they had felt. White caps melted into the grey cold water, and rose again – thousands of them. The gusts darkened the water as they ran. Up and down we went; riding the swell, watching as the clouds became greyer and the little pockets of blue disappeared. The horizon circled us, unbroken, nothing in the way. We were a small boat in the centre of an infinite circle of empty sea. The horizon never gets any nearer. The day went slowly and the miles slower. The wind was beginning to veer to the south so we changed our course and headed out to sea to keep our angle to the wind broad. The weather was beginning to deteriorate further.

The tiny bird constantly battled with the wind, tiny amid the vast desert of water ready to engulf him. He circled the boat for what seemed like an age to us and what must have be an age for his tired little wings. He was looking for refuge. He eventually landed on the deck and puffed like an exhausted marathon runner. He was not a sea bird but a lost swallow migrating south, much the same as we were I suppose. We were all glad that we could help him in his moment of need. And with that he took off again. It was just a fleeting visit – a little rest was all he wanted. We were sad to see him go somehow feeling that he wouldn't make it to land.

Things were continuing to break. First the self-steering, then the radar and the Genoa halyard. We did our best to repair the breakages but the electronics would have to wait until we were steady and in port. The radar was a big loss. It was an eye into the dark and had proved invaluable the night before for spotting and avoiding the squalls. We would have to manage. A persistent dampness covered everything down below – the seats, beds, clothes, everything. Nothing was getting a chance to dry. We all had wet backsides. The oilskins did their best to keep us dry but eventually gave up when we sat on the wet deck. My ass had now been wet for nearly thirty hours, I wondered would it ever dry out. Simon was great as skipper, keeping everyone in good spirits. He relished the challenge of the weather. He was tough, in a proud sort of way, and that rubbed off on the rest of us.

◊

We caught our first fish on the fourth day. At this stage we were not good fishermen so to catch a fish was a delight. The evening was calm, for the first time since we had left and a gentle swell was still there even though the wind had died down. The sun was setting and it had been a warm few hours. With relief we took the opportunity to dry out everything as best we could. The boat looked like a clothes-line, boxer shorts, sleeping bags and cushions were sprawled everywhere basking in the warm sun. We got another forecast, the worst yet – winds up to storm force ten! This was the so-called calm before the storm. Biscay was living up to its notorious reputation.

The ratchet on the reel spun furiously.

'It's a monster,' screamed Tony as he grabbed the rod, smiling from ear to ear, displaying our utter lack of angling coolness. He began to wind furiously. Andrew slowed the boat by pulling back the throttle on the engine to make it easier to pull in the line. The fish fought all the way to the stern of the boat, pulling one way and then the next, all against the line, the rod bending with the weight. Tony braced against the railing. He was fat, the fish that is, with a big lower jaw. Quite ugly. The hook had caught his upper row of teeth. He was exhausted by the time we got him into the bucket, as was Tony. There was a certain amount of panic once the fish was finally aboard, all of us too anxious to kill it. Tony decided the surest way of ending the misery was to stick one of his big catering knives into the fish's head. The sound was disgusting as the knife crunched through the gristle and the fish shuddered. Rebecca looked away – the rest of us watched with a primeval satisfaction. Tony, somewhat worryingly, enjoyed the whole thing. Before long what was a fish became a lump of meat on our wooden bread-board. The sun set over a blood-stained cockpit. Our first fish was in the fridge.

The fourth night was the first time any of us were really scared. There was lightning everywhere. We could see the brunt of the storm about twenty miles to the east of us. The flashes were blinding against the dark sky. We sat vulnerable, with a twenty metre aluminium mast sticking up in the air. The night passed without incident and when morning came all our spirits were down. The day was miserable – lashing rain and big seas, strong wind. The sky and water was almost one in a uniform greyness. All of us were tired and agreed that this was the worst day so far. Very little happened as we plodded south. Frictions began to surface over stupid things like music and tidiness.

◊

From a distance Bayona looked beautiful, the tan walls and red-tiled roofs of the old fort glowed in the autumn light. It was calm now as we passed Islas Cies, the islands just to the north of the town. The mountains hung behind the town, purple further away, greener nearer the port but still steep. Columbus arrived back here in 1493 returning from the New World, laden with riches and adventures, what a beautiful old port he chose. We slowly wound our way in through the buoyed channel. We were all in high spirits, the tiredness of the previous day re-placed with an excitement of someplace new. There were quite a few boats already in the sheltered harbour calmly rocking on their moorings. We quickly changed into our crew uniform, hoisted the Sail Chernobyl flag and radioed the port authorities. The port captain gave us a place at the pontoon.

We had arrived after five days and twenty-three hours. I must say we were all glad to be in. This first trip was a real eye-opener for all of us. We had encountered almost every weather condition and learned a lot about the boat, ourselves and what we were attempting to achieve. We had all managed in our own way over the last five days. Simon threw himself at the weather never letting it get to him, simply treating it as a challenge that had to be faced. Andrew busied himself with navigation and electrical repairs. Tony when not beavering in the workshop fixing things fed us all extraordinarily well in awful circumstances, each night producing a great dinner from the swaying galley. Rebecca had shown remarkable guts and never once flinched in the face of the gale. Her belief in Simon was total, always waking him at night if she felt worried about something. And me, well, I suppose I disguised my fears well, I was nervous particularly when the lightning exploded all around us. I think I could have said already that I wouldn't enjoy the nights at sea but it was just something I was going to have to get used to.

◊

'C'est quoi, Sail Chernobyl?' the French man on the boat next door shouted at me as I rinsed the deck down with fresh water, anxious to get the salt off. The afternoon sun was warm.

I looked over, somewhat startled by the tone of man. Judging from his appearance he seemed in his mid to late fifties. His bare upper body was very brown, shiny and saggy with age and the sea air. His hair was white and his face angry.

'Excuse me,' I replied hoping the man spoke English. The concept of Sail Chernobyl is difficult enough to explain in English without me trying to use my schoolboy French.

'Both me and my wife, have suffered greatly from Chernobyl,' he slowly said not that comfortable with English. 'We've both got cancer, of the thyroid, we hate Chernobyl, we hate nuclear, we live in the south of France and we still got sick,' he continued showing me the scar on his throat where the thyroid gland had been removed.

I quickly realised that the man thought that we were in someway promoting what had happened in Chernobyl.

'We hate what happened in Chernobyl also,' I said slowly so he could understand me. 'Sail Chernobyl is about trying to help the victims of this terrible disaster, particularly the children. We are working with an Irish-based charity that works in Belarus, the worst affected country. Each summer they bring children to Ireland for life-saving operations and recuperative holidays, and twice a year, in the autumn and spring, they send vital aid directly to the families and institutions that need it.'

I went on to explain what we were trying to do and about the further work that the charity does in western Russia and Belarus. I told him I could sympathise with him and his wife and that I had recently been to the Chernobyl region and had seen the children with the scars on their throats just like the one he had shown me moments earlier.

'Thank you,' he said, 'it's just the word, Chernobyl, it makes me very angry.'

Later I dropped him over the leaflet that described in more detail what we are doing and I gave him a copy of Adi Roche's book. He thanked me again and wished me luck on our voyage.

I was astounded at the incredible coincidence that the first person I met on our voyage was himself a victim of the Chernobyl disaster. People living as far away as the south of France could be directly affected.

◊

The streets were narrow behind the wide waterfront, cobbled and slippy in the evening dew. The air was warm and the place seemed sleepy and quiet. We quickly found a pub that seemed to have some life and before long we were fumbling in Spanish at the bar, trying to order. The barmaid was stunningly beautiful, tall with sallow skin and long bushy curly hair; she smiled enjoying our miserable attempts at communication. As none of us had a word of Spanish we ended up pointing at someone else's beer and she soon got the message. We looked a little conspicuous in the bar, quite obviously all from the same family, tall and definitely not Spanish.

It was odd really, quite unnatural. In the last few years I had never spent so much as a week with my four brothers and sister, and now we were to spend the next nineteen months together. Every day the five of us. A brother or sister relationship is always different. We tend to know too much about each other. Things that are intimate between friends are merely banal among siblings. There is a lack of tolerance, and a more complete understanding that lacks the respect or privacy of a standard friendship. Being out with your brothers and sister is always different than being out with your friends; at least I have always found it that way. This rather strange grouping of four brothers and a sister made me slightly nervous.

The second bar was far livelier and we soon discovered that the Spanish tended to go out late and as a result stay out much later than we do in Ireland. The bar was only warming up, starting to heave with europop and dark-haired people. I got chatting to two local men, one bearded, one small with glasses, about Ireland and what we are doing. I was told we were in a region called Galicia. Galitian nationalism is almost as passionate as the Basques but not as violent. These people identified more with the Portuguese than the Spanish. I remembered my childhood reading of *Asterix* and was told somewhat in jest that he is a hero in these parts. We all shuffled around on the dance floor for a bit, looking rather awkward, none of us are particularly good dancers, but at this stage none of us cared very much as the local brew had begun to take its toll. It was the first chance we had to relax in a long time. The month before we left had been hectic and the journey down to Bayona had been rough. We were all enjoying ourselves. The night ended late.

We began the repairs. It is surprising how quickly we were learning about the boat. There were so many things to worry about from hydraulics to sails to engines to food. We were enjoying the challenge of applying ourselves to the various repairs. Before long the deck was awash with tools of various descriptions. Simon sweated it out in the engine room, Tony tended to the varnishing, Rebecca mended the sail, Andrew had his face stuck in the fuse board, and I was riveting back the winch that had sheared from the mast in the storm. We all reckoned that by the time we returned home we would know everything there was to know about our boat.

Sunlight filled the cabin; it was the morning of our last day in Bayona. We had been there for nearly a week and we had all made good friends in Bayona. We were glad that we would be returning – the next time would be some eighteen months later

The bay looked beautiful as we rounded the southern headland, the white beach, red tiles and pale mountains falling away behind us. Evening came quickly, the sea calm and we were glad to be on the move again. It wasn't long before we were out of the sight of land. We had two beautiful days before the weather once again turned bad. In fact it was the two beautiful days that made the weather seem even worse. Having got used to the sun and the light winds from behind us the southerly gale depressed us. Soon it was like Biscay all over again. Everything was wet, the boat rocking violently in the swell, lightning again. The sky was very black during the nights, we couldn't see the waves, crash went the thunder, dazzling forks cracked the water, and we kept going south.

The morning of the fourth day we saw him. He surfaced like a great submarine behind the boat, looked about fifty feet long and a huge spout gushed from his blowhole. He was the first whale any of us had seen. Twenty feet behind the boat his huge back rolled out of the water, dark grey and slippery, he disappeared again. It's astonishing the lift the whale gave us. Seeing one of the great creatures of the world so close and so completely wild and free cheered us up immensely. We are all in awe of the huge monster from the deep, breaking the grey water. He didn't hang around for long and by the time Andy got hold of the video camera he was gone. It was a little like the Kit-Kat advertisement with the pandas in the zoo.

◊

First we saw bamboo sticks floating, then leaves and then the birds. We couldn't yet see Porto Santo because the clouds were so low and dark on the horizon.

'I think I see it,' cried Andrew in the classic sort of land ahoy way, eye-sockets bruised from the binoculars.

'It's the only cloud that isn't moving,' he qualified

Porto Santo emerged out of the sky like something out of *Jurassic Park*. Tall and austere, the dark cliff-faces jutted skyward just distinguishable from the greyness. We were delighted to see it. Originally we had planned to go straight to Las Palmas from Bayona, but the weather had driven us to look for shelter earlier and Porto Santo or Madeira were the obvious choices. As we came around the north-eastern tip of the island, the wind strengthened and the white horses raced and crashed against the rugged shoreline. We could see the breakwater of the harbour; the entrance was small, inside there were many boats sheltering. Out to sea we could see the German boat that had left Bayona the same time as us, they had obviously decided to push on for Madeira. They were getting a hammering from the squall, pitching and rolling – we were glad it wasn't us. We dropped the anchor once inside the harbour, glad to have found shelter. We were all exhausted and wet.

The wind blew the red dust down from the steep crumbling cliff-face that stood around the harbour like a wall. The breakwater, circling us on the seaward side, was covered with drawings and graffiti. There was very little in the way of buildings, just a wide road, that led to the ferry terminal, covered in the red earth and rocks from a recent landslide. There was a small bar full of over-tanned travellers, the brown tan ingrained and weathered on to their faces. David was the harbour master, he was English, tall and looks like Mel Gibson in *Mad Max*, and in fact the whole place looked like the film set of *Mad Max*, dry red earth, weathered land and people. The water was turquoise despite the grey sky, the pale sand underneath bleaching the blue.

Simon and myself decided to walk to the town, about three miles away, to get some fresh bread and milk. The beach stretched around the bay, the white sand was dotted with dark rocks, bleached wood and seaweed. It was good to get away from the boat for a while.

From the small town a jetty jutted out over the water. We walked out and agreed that it was a classic girlfriend snogging place. Then we saw a couple kissing. The two of us had been missing our girlfriends and talked about them on and off. What's going to happen, is it the end, the usual sort of male stuff, going round in circles, never really coming to any conclusions, always ending up with 'we'd be better off without them', and not really meaning it. We jumped off the pier, in a jealous effort to ruin the couple's solitude with our splashing.

When we woke the following morning the wind had strengthened considerably. The previous evening we had moved next to the quay and tied on to fill up with water and plug into the mains. The wind was blowing a force 7–8 from the south-west. Waves were crashing against the breakwater and the spray was coming over the wall in misty spurts. The ferry was unable to come in; the waves at the entrance to the harbour were too big. We all went up to see the ship rolling violently in the swell, the poor passengers, having puked their way across the forty miles from Madeira, now had to turn around and do it all over again with no respite. Shortly after the ferry disappeared all became calm and then as suddenly as the wind dropped it veered to the north and strengthened to storm force 10. The gusts came rattling down the cliffs behind the harbour, the water turned dark and the rain lashed down the hatch of the boat. There was mayhem in the harbour. Boats were being blown everywhere, caught by the surprise. Two got entangled and were being blown out to sea. We had our own problems – the boat started to bash against the wall. The five of us frantically began to tie more ropes to the quay and got more fenders and tyres to stop the boat from hitting the wall. The boat swung with each gust and the fenders squashed against the quay. The sound of the wind had become unbearable. The two boats that were careering through the harbour were lucky not to have hit the breakwater, and were very quickly about half a mile out to sea. One of the boats was owned by elderly Swiss couple who we met the previous night. The harbour master heroically managed to get on board their boat and give them well-needed assistance. The other boat, Swedish, was also out there and both boats were waiting for the winds to calm down before attempting to come back in. The gusts kept coming all day, with each one *Golden Apple* lurched against the wall, testing the ropes and the fenders.

The following day the wind calmed down. We were anxious to head off again as we were due in Las Palmas in a few days. Two days later the winds had calmed enough for us to head off. The crossing to the Canary Islands was a great one; the winds were behind us all the way. We arrived in Las Palmas on 8 November passing the snow-capped Pico de Teide of Tenerife at dawn. It was dark by the time we were tied up; the lights of the city were glimmering on the water.

3

Our First Big Ocean

Las Palmas bustled, as much as Spanish cities can, sleeping in the afternoon. It was a much bigger place than I had imagined it to be. That first morning, after we had docked the boat properly, I decided to take a walk through the town to post some letters. It was nice to be on my own away from the others for a while; it was the first time I had left the boat on my own in over a month. Las Palmas is broken into a new and old quarter; the old part of the town is very beautiful with its crumbling facades and tree-filled plazas. People seemed to move quite slowly as if they had nothing to do and although it was November it was still warm under the shade of the trees. I like post offices in foreign countries and grew to like them more as the trip progressed. They are places where you can see all sorts of people, from the locals who are paying bills, to travellers like me who are sending postcards and letters to people they care about. For me it's nice to think that people have someone they care enough about to let them know how they are getting on. With all the advances in modern communications nothing has replaced the excitement of receiving a letter, particularly from someone who is far away. You can never tell people enough that you love them, and it's good to just let them know you are thinking of them. The new part of town was less appealing with lots of tourists in really awful neon shorts and staying in tacky modern hotels. They all seemed to be so preoccupied with buying ice creams and T-shirts that it didn't seem like they were having a holiday at all. I suppose everyone has a different way of relaxing. The beach was crowded with red-skinned people desperately seeking that mid winter tan.

There were many boats at the Meulle Deportivo, the port complex, preparing for the Atlantic crossing as we were. The crossing was going to be our first big ocean passage and we were all a little nervous. The previous weeks while they had been tough enough were relatively short hops, five days at the longest. This next journey was going to be nearly 3,000 miles, close to three weeks at sea with nothing around us. We were entered in the ARC race and were glad to be part of a group of boats going across together – if we did get into trouble at least there would be someone relatively near us. The ARC race leaves Las Palmas every year towards the end of November, most boats deciding, like we had, that they didn't want to cross the Atlantic on their own.

There was a tremendous cosmopolitan flavour in the harbour with flags from all over Europe, Australia and the United States fluttering from the boats. There were all types of boats, old and new, ugly and elegant, big and tiny, and on them were equally diverse people. From the lean blond-headed Scandinavians to the fat, bearded Texans, all were sharing the common goal of preparing to cross the world's second largest ocean. The people on either side of us were great. Phil was working on a big English boat next to us called *Thunder.* The owner of the boat had not arrived yet so Phil was getting everything ready. Phil is English, from the north I think. On the other side we had a German called Thom. Thom smoked a lot; in fact he is one of the few people I have met that consistently smoked more than me. Every second of the day he was smoking. He is a real veteran, late thirties and had worked on boats all his life. He and a friend of his run a sailing school in Germany. He spoke perfect English, had sun bleached hair, and generally looked dishevelled. We proudly flew our Irish flag. We worked tirelessly on the boat; the varnish work had got very shabby-looking over the summer. With the other things to do we did not get time to look after it. Andrew and Tony attacked it with vigour, constantly comparing *Golden Apple* with the super yachts, in an almost obsessive way. Varnishing was to become a feature of the trip particularly as the sun became hotter, we had to redo it over and over again. Simon and I worked in the engine room.

Mum, Dad and our brother David arrived the week before we were due to leave. Two friends also came to wish us the best, Simon's girlfriend Ruth and Rose, a good friend of mine. We really appreciated them coming out and giving us a hand with the preparations. Unfortunately it didn't turn out to be much of a holiday for them as we were so busy getting ready for the crossing.

David was to join the boat for the crossing to the Caribbean. Mum and Dad had talked a lot about whether to let him come or not and finally decided that it was a chance of lifetime for him and one that he might never get again. Of course it was a risk but no more than it was for the rest of us. We were a little apprehensive about letting him come but we, like our parents, agreed that it would be good for him. He has always found it difficult being the youngest by a good few years and Sail Chernobyl was something that he hadn't really been part of. I think he was delighted to be involved in this leg and as we all worked to get the boat ready he really began to feel part of the crew.

Both our parents were a great help in getting things ready for the crossing. Dad was very meticulous and scrutinised every inch of the boat for possible weaknesses and annoyingly took great pride in pointing things out to us that we had overlooked or not noticed. I think he found it a little hard that he was not going on the crossing. It is something I know he would have dearly loved to do and he even said to Mum that he thought that the two of them should maybe do it in a few years' time. Mum helped Tony and Rebecca with the stocking up of food and other essentials for life at sea.

Tony being the cook was given the task of provisioning for the trip. It was a difficult job to work out how much six people will eat for a period of up to three weeks. He had become very dependent on a small freezer that we carry on board to keep fresh meat. Unlike a conventional house, space on a boat is at a premium so storage of everything has to be meticulously planned. The other problem is of course the movement of the boat so we have to ensure that everything is secure, particularly heavy things like cans of food which could hurt someone if they started flying all over the place. Our diet was restricted to things that will last – for the first few days we have fresh vegetables and fruit but on a long passage they will only keep for four to five days and after that it is the canned and dried stuff. Fresh fish was also a welcome addition when we were able to catch it.

There are some interesting ways for keeping fruit and vegetable fresh. Planting carrots in soil was just one insight although we didn't try it for fear of cockroach infestation, an unpleasant thing on a boat. Cockroaches aren't really something Irish people are used to and for us they were an entirely new problem. On a boat they have nowhere to go once they get on and they will continue to breed until there are thousands of them. They tend to lay their eggs in cardboard so as the boxes of food arrived to the dock all the cardboard had to be left on the shore. Vegetables and fruit also had to be washed individually. As far as we could see no cockroaches made it onto the boat. After many trips around the town to the various supermarkets and much washing and careful storing we were all stocked up.

From the moment we arrived in Las Palmas we began preparing to have a fundraising party for all the competitors. We realised before we left that it was always going to be difficult to organise events around the world where we would be guaranteed a crowd. The ARC was an exception as we were part of a ready-made group of competitors. There was a lot of interest in Sail Chernobyl, people were constantly coming up and asking about it. We approached the organisers of the ARC and asked if it would be possible to have a fundraising night in the week leading up to the departure of all the boats. We had sponsorship from Murphy's Irish Stout who would supply all the drinks for the evening, so we felt, if for no other reason than free drink, people would come to hear what we had to say regarding Chernobyl. I know this is a rather cynical view but the important thing was to try to get them there, and then it was up to us to impress them. In the days preceding it we canvassed as many of the boats as we could to ensure a big turn out. Rebecca was particularly good at it and convinced many of the owners to come along. It went really well on the night and it turned out to be the biggest event of the week. Everyone seemed to enjoy themselves and many were genuinely interested in what we were trying to achieve in terms of fundraising. We raised nearly £2,000 with promises of much more so it was definitely worth the effort.

◊

We were ready to head to the high seas for the longest voyage of the entire journey. It was very calm at the start of the race. All the boats barely drifted over the start line and headed south. We had been told by the weather forecaster that the best winds were to be found to the south, near the equator, so most boats headed in that direction before going west towards St Lucia some 3,000 miles away. We got a really good start and as the first night fell we picked up some good wind in near the shore. We were heeled over beautifully and were well ahead of most of the fleet. After the first three days it was remarkable how quickly the fleet had split up. We couldn't see anyone and didn't again for another ten days.

Little things can become big things on a boat. There was always a drip, or rather a dribble. It was the same with both of them. Simon and Andrew. Every morning since we left it had been the same. The spoon scooped the dribble of milk from their stubbly chins. Then another spoonful. Greasy noses and milky chins, the first five minutes of every day. Cornflakes. Tony was different, he was neater and more proper but he does have a rather annoying habit of taking huge mouthfuls of food and really swinging his jaw around. Rebecca just looked cross; she was always cross in the morning like me. It doesn't matter how long she has been sleeping. She too had the greasy nose, I think it must run in the family. I'd never noticed these things before this trip. But on the boat the space was so small, a dribble of milk became a waterfall, sitting on the chin waiting to be scooped.

I was the first to see these things; I slept above the table. It was worse when the weather was bad, because I wasn't feeling the best anyway, with the swaying. I suppose I was seeing everyone at their worst, half-clad and sweaty. I have never enjoyed watching people eat no matter what time of day. I have always been self-conscious about it myself, particularly if there is someone next to me who is not eating. That's why I notice. The sound is worse than the actions, the munching and cleaning of teeth with tongue. It's not that I am blaming anyone, I probably look the same. I confronted Simon and he just said, 'why don't you just get up earlier?' I suppose he had a point. It's the small things that will get on your nerves, not the big things. After three days on the transatlantic crossing I realised for the first time what it was like to live in such a small space and what it was going to be like for the rest of the journey. The little things you would never notice in ordinary circumstances become magnified. I was relieved it was only my brothers and sister as it would be more difficult with other people. I am sure each of the others had things that annoyed them; well annoyed would be the wrong word – more like irritated. People's idiosyncrasies had nowhere to hide; some are reassuring and make me laugh. The way Andrew would frown when he was concentrating on something difficult or how Tony would walk around a piece of varnish work and congratulate himself. Rebecca always had a funny way of saying 'nine' and Simon had a ridiculous machismo when it came to physical things. On the whole all these things added up to the character of the whole boat.

Dave was very nervous from the beginning and very cautious. It took him a while to get used to the idea of living on the boat but after a few days at sea he was great to have on board. He had been set schoolwork by his teachers to complete before he got back so that he wouldn't fall too far behind. After a while he settled into the routine of doing his work in the mornings and then taking it easy in the afternoons. Dave is a great conversationalist, one on one, when you take the time to listen to what he has to say. It has always been difficult for him in such a big family to get a word in but now it was different. I would always try to get him up to do watches at night with me as he would often bring up the most obscure thoughts and ideas. He would sit in front of the wheel while I steered and talk away under the stars. Often it would be about football or school or his favourite topic of girls. For a 13-year-old he was pretty up to speed on the whole girl thing and he would only be looking for an older perspective on what he knew already but just needed to be reassured. Sometimes he would take on more complex themes out of the blue, one minute he be talking about the skills of Eric Cantona and then suddenly out of nowhere he would hop to 'did I think there was aliens out there?' He was, and is, a lazy sod however and when it came to doing chores on the boat like the wash-up after dinner it was like getting blood from a stone. In an effort to try to shake some of this out of him we decided to do some exercises each day and by the end of the crossing we had got Dave from one miserable press-up to nearly twenty.

He was great for Rebecca as well. The two of them had always been very close and I think she had missed him a lot. In many ways Rebecca was being forced to grow up faster than would ordinarily be the case on this trip and he was a welcome relief from her older brothers. Dave also proved to be the best fisherman on the crossing, albeit with some rather unorthodox methods. We were using lures that looked like small squids and having no luck until he caught the only fish of the trip on the second last day. He decided we had to change something so he made his own lure and wrote little messages on it like 'kiss me, I'm sexy' and 'eat me, you handsome devil'. It obviously worked as we caught a three-foot Wahoo minutes later. Of course he never let us forget it.

For someone who has never done a long passage at sea it is difficult to explain what it is like and indeed what it was like for most of the journey around the world. Try to imagine sitting on a very slow train with the same people for nearly three weeks, looking out of a window that never changes except from light to dark. Endless hours of sameness. You see the sea doesn't change very much. Of course the weather changes but very often it stays the same for days. I know this doesn't sound like the adventure of a life-time but that is the way it was for most of the time. The landfalls were what made the journeys worthwhile. I, and I think all of us, craved change while we were at sea even if there was an element of danger in it. To catch a fish, a sudden gust of wind or rain squall, or of course some sea-life was wonderful and lifted everyone, but

these were often few and far between. The important thing was to try to keep busy and occupy your mind. Each of us had different ways of dealing with the boredom. Andy usually immersed himself in something to do with the boat, some device that wasn't working properly – he would spend hours taking something apart and putting it back together in order to understand it. Tony would usually make things out of wood that added to the aesthetics of the boat, or spend time varnishing or painting. Rebecca, like me, would read.

We were lucky to be part of a race for this our longest leg and it did add a great deal of competition. It wasn't really a competitive race but rather a rally with the aim of a safe crossing for everyone. Of course we didn't really see it as this. Everyone on our boat was competitive. All of us had represented Ireland in some sport or other. I think it stemmed from our Dad who was very competitive and had always encouraged us to be so. We not only wanted to make it safely across to the Caribbean but also to beat as many of the other boats there as possible. We played a vital part in the race over the three weeks. We were one of a small number of link boats for the fleet. With 150 boats in the race, communication was very important and we were one of the main links in the communication chain between the outside world and all the competitors. A lot of the communications were channelled through us and we relayed them via email to the race centre in Cowes, Isle of Wight. The messages included weather forecasts and updates on the position of each yacht and any problems that people were having. Each morning we conducted the role-call for boats in our group and they told us their positions so it was easy to plot their locations on the chart and see how we were doing and, of course, which boats were close by. We could also see where the best winds were judging from the boats ahead and behind. We had to help with a variety of difficulties, or at least act as a communication

centre to try to resolve some of the problems on other boats. One of the crew members on a boat called *Kanaloa* cut his toe really badly and we had to talk to a doctor and then relay the instructions to the skipper on how best to perform the necessary stitches. There was some rather funny situations also. One boat had the misfortune of being covered in human excrement from a passing jumbo jet shortly after leaving Las Palmas. Their entire boat, sails and crew were covered in a foul-smelling brown sludge, which they had to endure for the remainder of their crossing. The best thing about all the radio work was that we made many friends on the airwaves who we couldn't wait to meet once we arrived in St Lucia. It was enjoyable trying to imagine what the people were like having talked to them for nearly three weeks. Simon or Andrew usually did the radio work with Rebecca doing it sometimes. Tony and myself never did, the two us both hate the telephone so the radio wasn't really going to be our thing. I just don't really like talking into machines be they answering machines or the intercom at a drive-through McDonalds.

Two days out from St Lucia we celebrated Andy and Tony's twenty-first birthday. It was a little hard for them to be out in the middle of nowhere for their birthday and we had hoped we would be ashore. We had a bit of a party for them – Simon cooked some brownies and I fried up the steaks we had saved especially for the day. Mum and Dad had given Rebecca some presents and cards in Las Palmas which were a real surprise for them. We caught sight of another boat that day for the first time in over a week. We radioed them and told them that we were celebrating a twenty-first and would they like to come over for a few beers. It was a Norwegian boat and as it turned out they too were celebrating a birthday. It was a calm day so we tied up next to them for an hour or so out there in the middle of nowhere. One of the crew played the accordion so

we had a great sing-song before heading off again. I think the lads enjoyed their somewhat unconventional twenty-first party.

One of the best things about travelling like this is that I really began to look forward to arriving in new places. Few places could be more exciting to visit than the Caribbean. The last time I had been there I was four and only had a very vague memory of it. It was a family holiday and we were on a boat, a catamaran called *Superstar.* I can remember swimming with my bare little ass bobbing above the water and the big orange armbands holding me up. I would float there and peer down at the wonderful fish through a small blue mask. I remember I found the snorkel difficult to use and kept putting my head too far under so it would fill with water. This time I was twenty years older and couldn't wait to get there again.

St Lucia came into view from quite a way out. Tony actually started crying when we saw the lush green mountains. It was unlike him but I suppose we all felt that a major hurdle was over when we saw the island. We had crossed the Atlantic Ocean, our first large ocean and we were now well and truly far away from both Europe and Ireland. As we rounded the point into Rodney Bay the wind strengthened and we heeled right over and we could see the masts of the other boats in the harbour. Before long we had the sails down and were tied to the dock after nineteen days at sea. We were the twenty-second boat to arrive and the party had already begun. We were greeted on the dock in true Caribbean style with steel band music and rum punch and scantily-clad local girls with flowers in their hair.

4

A Whole New World

We were all relieved to be off the boat and it was great to meet so many new people and to put faces to those we had spoken to on the radio everyday for nearly three weeks.

The little street was packed with people. The music was as loud as it could be. Virtually everyone was black. Every Friday night was the 'Jump up'; a street party in one of the local areas of St Lucia near Rodney Bay where all the boats from the ARC race were gathered. The five of us, along with some of the other crews, decided to go there as it was our first night ashore since Las Palmas and we were all anxious to have a good time.

The music was loud, the locals loved it and the sweat rolled down their bare backs, it was like a sexual ritual as they danced and wove in and out of one another. It was fantastic to see so many people unashamedly having fun and really enjoying themselves. It was very refreshing having lived in trendy Dublin – enthusiasm and an appetite for fun is so much more attractive than an apparent coolness that simply shrouds conservatism. Along the sides of the road everything was being sold from drinks to gifts to all types of local food. We danced and joined in as best we could although our rather poor sense of rhythm was highlighted once again by the local people. There was, and is, an edge to the whole thing. As a white person I did feel a little uncomfortable, it's not that anyone consciously was aggressive towards us but more like we were simply so out of place that it felt a little strange. Ironically the bar was called 'The Golden Apple' the same name as our boat and looked to me like a bordello from one of those old westerns with balconies and white cotton curtains blowing in the warm wind. It was as different from a night out at home as it could be. The street party went on well into the early hours and it was nearly bright before we all managed to stumble back to the boat.

We met Eric for the first time in St Lucia. The reason I mention him is that he was to spend the next four months on and off with us. Simon, Rebecca and I were sitting in the restaurant and were doing an interview with *Yachting World,* a sailing magazine. An old-looking man approached us from another table and asked if we would all like to join him on his boat for drinks and dinner afterwards. He seemed a very nice man with a lovely old wooden boat who just admired what we were doing. The five of us arrived around eight o'clock and to our surprise the first thing Eric did was give Simon a cheque for £1,000. It was as if by doing this he was very anxious that we take him seriously. He turned out to be quite different from what we expected. He told us that he had started working with a small firm in Munich, when he was 23, specialising in the manufacturing of sausage skins. He had retired a year previously and the company of which he had become managing director employed over 19,000 people worldwide. His boat was meticulous in every detail and beautifully finished, it was obvious that he loved it almost irrationally, everything was perfect and the very best quality. Over dinner he turned out to be one of those annoying people with an eclectic knowledge of almost anything. His most recent venture was the breeding of thoroughbred cattle on a farm in Tasmania.

I don't think he liked me a whole lot from the beginning. I tend to joke with people a little when I meet them first, particularly if they are taking everything so seriously and I am not sure if he took too kindly to this. His boat was named after a Danish warrior called Holger Danske and as he was telling us the rather long-winded story of this mythical figure I made a few jokes which I don't think he found very amusing. At first I didn't really like him a whole lot either. It's not that I didn't respect and admire what he had achieved but more that I didn't like his manner. He had been very generous to us and we thought it would be a good idea, as he was going the same direction as us, to meet up with him again at Panama and go through the canal together.

Our parents arrived out a few days before Christmas. They were to spend a few weeks with us and we had all been looking forward to their arrival. They came laden down with presents and good wishes from our friends at home. Dad inspected his boat with a fine comb, as only he could, looking for things that might be damaged. As we headed off to explore some of the islands I think he found it difficult to accept that we now knew a lot more about his boat than he did and how independent we had become. It was amusing to us when he announced that he didn't want to be involved in any of the decisions but merely be a guest on the boat. We all knew that he would be incapable of this and before long he was making all the plans as to where we would go over the next few weeks.

It's hard not to be nostalgic about that holiday with Dad and Mum, it was to be the last time we were to have with him and I suppose that inevitably clouds the fact that he was, over those three weeks, a bit of a pain in the ass. He always loved antagonising each of us by provoking arguments between us. It wasn't malicious it was just his way of bugging us. He would joke that I was lazy, that Simon was disorganised, that Andy was too serious, and that Tony and Bec were too sensitive and derived great enjoyment in rising us. Over the years Simon and Dad used to argue a lot but Simon had learned to control himself and as skipper he just let Dad do what he wanted rather than allowing himself be provoked into a fight.

Christmas dinner was a bit of a squash, with eight of us on

the boat. Tony had managed to find a turkey he could fit into our tiny gas oven, although he did have to cut off the legs to fit it in. He prepared a great feast and we all crowded around the table in the cabin. We even had plum pudding. We all wore those stupid hats that come in the crackers. Mum was determined to have the boat looking like it was Christmas, so she brought out decorations and fake holly to put up everywhere. We even had the canned snow sprayed onto the windows, which was a little ridiculous as we were sitting in the Caribbean. It was a shame Patrick wasn't there for that last Christmas dinner together as a whole family.

After Christmas day we headed south through the Lesser Antilles Islands towards Grenada. Mum, Dad and Dave were due to fly back to Ireland on 7 January from there. We spent New Year in the small whaling island of Bequia. The journey from St Lucia to Bequia was an overnight sail. In the early morning before we arrived it was flat calm and Andy, Dad and I were up on watch. We were chatting and watching the sun rise above the big island of St Vincent when all of a sudden, about two hundred yards ahead of us, a school of about forty dolphins were jumping together in a straight line and flying towards us. It was a wonderful sight as they passed either side of us. They are the very essence of freedom.

There was a fantastic atmosphere in Bequia as most of the boats from the ARC had decided to stop there. New Year's Eve was one huge party with lots of Caribbean rum and steel band music. It was the last time that we were going to see most of the people. Very few of the ARC boats were carrying on around the world, and most of those that would be going would be taking much longer than us. We said our farewells and the following day we headed off.

We stopped in Palm Island on the way to Grenada. Palm Island was a small little resort island where Mum and Dad had stayed many times over the years when they went away on holidays together. It was owned by an eccentric American who while trying to sail around the world had ended up there and never left. Dad had always dreamed of bringing his own boat there and couldn't really believe that we were there in his own *Golden Apple*. We had a wonderful few nights and were treated with the rare sight of Dad jiving with Mum to some local dance tunes. I think we all realised where our lack of dance floor flair and rhythm stemmed from.

Mum, Dad and David went home in the early hours of the seventh. It was an emotional goodbye as they didn't know when they would next see us. We had no idea that it was going to be the last time we were to see Dad. It's strange that one never really knows when it will be the last of anything. He had been bugging me throughout the whole holiday about the book and I promised to send him the first few chapters before we passed through the Panama Canal. Luckily he got them a day before he died. It's just a shame he will never see the published book.

We were now back to five and as far as we were concerned it was back to work. We were going to miss Dave. It was back to school for him but he didn't seem to mind too much. We would all miss him – he had been kind of comic relief for all of us at times, although there was nothing humorous about his smelly clothes and the endless times he left our walkmans to melt in the sun on the deck. Apart from those little faults he had been a great success and in some ways it was a pity he wasn't doing the whole trip.

We had about a week in Grenada before we were due to head off towards Venezuela. We took the time to catch up on boat maintenance that had been neglected over the previous three weeks. We had a list of things we needed to get done before we set sail again. I'll give you an idea of the sort of stuff we had to do; change the oil and fuel filters in the engine, stitch and patch damaged sails, clean and grease all moving parts on board, varnish all the wood that had faded in the sun, charge spare batteries, patch up our punt (tender) which had taken a hammering in the previous three weeks, service the outboard engine, clean out all the food lockers and restock for the voyage, refuel, give all the ropes and rigging a thorough examination to check for wear, tear or stress marks, generally tidy and clean to keep the boat looking good and habitable. I know this may sound like a lot but with five of us working we managed to get through it quickly. Constant repairs were part of a trip like this, as there was constant stress and wear on the hull, sails and rigging during long passages at sea. All we could do was try to minimise the potential problems with constant inspection and maintenance. It was a real challenge to us and crucial if we were to complete the voyage safely and within our budget. Andy and I spent some rather hot and greasy days in the engine room.

We also got back to work on raising the awareness of Chernobyl. We visited the Presentation Brothers school in St Georges, the capital of Grenada, to talk to three brothers there – one is Irish, Brother Matthias Comyns from Clare – and some of the students. The visit was a huge success. We spoke to two separate classes about the accident in Chernobyl and visited the school yard at break time where we were surrounded by students. The children were fascinated by the boat trip and afterwards about sixty of them came down to the boat to see for themselves what it was like. Later on in the voyage it was going to be children that raised most of the money for the Sail Chernobyl project, especially in Ireland. We also managed to get on Grenadan national television and the interview went well. They did a very good job and added in original footage of the Chernobyl nuclear accident.

The idea of arriving in South America was one I had been looking forward to since we had begun planning this whole voyage. This continent for me conjured up images of sleazy drug barons called Carlos and guns and beautiful women, mountain ranges and jungles, snakes and piranhas. This dangerous element was confirmed for us when we met a couple of Americans who told us of their experiences off the Colombian coast. A brother of one of the New Yorkers had been sailing close to the coast when they were attacked by pirates. The brother and his wife were slashed savagely with machetes and everything on the boat was robbed. They were very lucky not to have been killed. While all this sounded horrendous and dangerous, it was, as a good friend of mine would say, intriguing. It had never before really crossed my mind that we might be in danger like that. We were heading into the unknown and while these movie and story-based images were exiting we really didn't have a clue what to expect.

Having sailed through the night we arrived safely at the remote islands of Los Testigos – yes I know it is an unfortunate name. This small group of islands lies some 35 miles off the coast of Venezuela. There are only 160 natives on the islands, all fishermen and their families. The only visitors they get are boats like us since there's no ferry or plane to the islands. We received a warm welcome from the coastguard officer who was very interested in our Spanish translated leaflet about Sail Chernobyl and the Chernobyl Children's Charity. This was the only way we could explain to him who we were and where we had come from as none of us could speak any Spanish.

These people led a peasant-style existence. They lived along the beach in small houses and their life was based around the sea. The crystal clear water was teeming with fish of all kinds. The landscape was nearly all rocky much like parts of Connemara except the stone had a reddish colour. In many ways it was like a desert with giant cacti being the principal vegetation. We were approached many times by some of the younger fishermen looking to trade freshly-caught lobsters for cigarettes and cans of beer. There were no shops of any kind so for these people any manufactured goods had to be brought from the mainland and were a real luxury. We stayed for two days and climbed the island's highest peak in search of the giant iguanas that we were told by the coastguard were quite common in the hills.

The resort island of Margarita was our next stop before reaching the mainland. It was about as different from Los Testigos as you could imagine. Massive high-rise apartment blocks and hotels and lots of neon lights. It fitted a little closer to my expectations of sleaze and corruption. Ancient looking Chevrolets and other battered American style cars roamed the streets. When you look at the passing cars, gigantic bonnets, alloy wheels and dark tinted windows you feel as if you're in a scene from *The Godfather.* Amid all the street bustle, we stumbled across a McDonalds. We couldn't stop ourselves from entering. We savoured our first familiar taste of a Big Mac since leaving home. Our disastrous knowledge of Spanish caused several embarrassing moments. In an attempt to communicate we were regularly forced to draw pictures for shopkeepers, while other customers just laughed. Simple tasks like buying some bread or even an ice cream led to all sorts of complications.

Strangely my most vivid memory of the place was not the sleaze but moreover the battle I had with our toilet. I broke it, no, not in the act of using it but in trying to service it I broke the main plunge pump. Unlike conventional house toilets, on a boat, you have to pump everything into the water using either an electric pump or, as in our case, a manual pump. The toilet was put into the boat when it was built some twenty years ago and as a result the parts for it are very hard to get, particularly where we were. I had to get it fixed or else we would be faced with the unpleasant prospect of using a bucket. I spent two days searching for a welder who could re-weld the bronze plunger back together. Bronze welding is a delicate business and I soon discovered it was as much an art as a trade. Luckily I found a taxi driver who seemed to understand both what I was looking for and the urgency of the problem. After we had scoured the back streets and talked to several dodgy welding shop-owners we finally managed to find an old man capable of doing the task. To celebrate the two of us went to a bar for a drink and proudly displayed the mended plunger for the barman. Once my taxi man explained the nature of the victory, he proceeded to pour us a few free beers. It's amazing the things that stand out about a place.

On reaching the mainland of Venezuela, for the first time since leaving Cork, we left the boat unattended and headed inland to explore the unknown. Our adventure began at 05.00 in the morning when we were picked up by our guide and driver in their 'A-Team' van. A six-hour drive, through oil fields and then marsh and jungle, brought us to a tiny village situated on a tributary to the giant Orinoco River. We couldn't really believe we had come the whole way from the tiny Minane Bridge river next to our house in Cork to the Orinoco in Venezuela.

Local Indian children played on the roadside and stopped to view us with curiosity. They were beautiful dark children and they smiled as I tried to capture them with my camera. The five of us with our guide and a local fisherman boarded a small motor boat to start our journey downstream. The river was mucky brown. Both banks were covered with dense jungle. The constant biting of flies and giant insects was unbearable. For some reason they seemed to enjoy our white Irish skin as they ignored both our guide and boat driver. Rebecca

sprayed herself non-stop with repellent. But it was useless.

Every half mile or so along the bank there was an isolated Indian hut, made only from tree branches with leaves on the roofs. There were no walls on these shelters, just a roof and a platform on stilts above the river's flooding level. In most cases the natives were relaxing in hammocks as we went by. The people themselves were very small, and seemed even smaller surrounded by us. They had jet-black hair and their skin was a dark brown. Some of them seemed somewhat resentful of us, although I am not really surprised as when we passed many of them in their dug-out log canoes our driver refused to slow down and almost capsized them as they paddled frantically to keep steady.

One of the huts appeared to be a school. It contained a blackboard and a few chairs. Apparently the local children go to class three months of the year, mainly to learn Spanish. It was very basic. A little boy proudly showed us his chair. These children were so unaware of the world outside their own. They had no outside influences, except the odd boat with people like us, there was no television, no radio or newspapers. I wondered what would become of them, would they ever leave this world of the river and jungle?

On our return journey we stopped to fish for piranha. We were hopeless at it. However the fisherman with us did manage to catch one. Its teeth were vicious. Our guide held it up and put a leaf in front of it and the little fish munched straight through the leaf. We could see the rows of tiny razor sharp teeth, apparently like sharks these fish can grow back broken teeth within a matter of hours. We certainly weren't going to go for a swim despite our guide telling us it was safe.

Back in the van, we travelled five hours through mountains to the small town of Caripe where we spent the night. It was a rich coffee-growing region and we could smell it as we

drove. The accommodation was far from extravagant, but our first night in a decent bed since leaving Ireland made it seem like luxury. It felt really good to be in a bed and we all slept soundly.

The following day we were heading for caves in the mountains. The Guacharo cave, being eight miles long, is one of the world's longest and most magnificent. We were guided by a pygmy-like man, with a dim oil lamp, into the darkness of the cave. Although very dark there was no lack of activity inside. It is inhabited by some 18,000 Guacharo birds, strange creatures not unlike bats but much noisier. The floor was littered with millions of seeds that the birds fed on, having brought them in from outside the cave. Even the least edgy of us, Simon, felt a little uncomfortable at the sight of a moving ground with all the cricket-like creatures and maggots. We fought on however and witnessed some really beautiful rock formations, stalagmites and stalactites. We all found it amusing that our guide seemed always to point out the most erotic images in the rocks. I think he may have been trying to impress Rebecca, she was disgusted by the dirty little man.

We only stayed another few days in Venezuela before heading off towards Panama. On our way we stopped in the very special islands of Los Roques. This small cluster of islands is a group of sandy beaches perched on top of coral reefs. There was only one substantial island on which there was a small resort town. We had a good few days here but there was one strange sight. We were anchored in a small lagoon where there were no other boats and no people living on the island near us. The five of us decided to walk around the island and as we were stumbling along the coral rocks we came upon what looked like a dog kennel. The walls were white-washed and it had a Spanish style red-tiled roof, much like all the buildings in the town we had been in the previous night. There was a little door on what

was quite clearly a tomb or grave by the withered flowers that were lying around the entrance. I opened the door and looked inside. There was a glow inside and to my surprise there was a lighted candle, the flame of which now flickered in the draft. I could see a photograph of a young man. He was dressed in what looked to me like a bullfighting uniform, a short black jacket gilded around the lapels. Judging from the photo he could not have been much older than me. Surrounding the photo lay an assortment of things from a watch to a small penknife. It amazed me that there was a lighted candle. There was no one living on the island, and the candle could only last at best for a day. It was beautiful, if sad, to imagine this young man's, father, mother or young wife, rowing five or six miles everyday to keep the candle burning for their lost loved one. Further down the beach we found the wreck of a small boat and assumed that he must have drowned on that rocky shore.

5

To the Enchanted Islands

Most people who visit Panama only ever go to the canal which is centred around the massive Panama city. About seventy miles south of the entrance to the canal lie the San Blas Islands. We had arranged to meet Eric and *Holger Danske* here. We arrived about three days before Eric and took some time to explore. The three of us walked down the beach as the sun was setting in the late afternoon. It was about the most idyllic beach ever, with coconut trees bending low over the sand and out over the turquoise water. Along the shore the little Kuna men were mending their nets and off-loading masses of conch shells from their small dug-out canoes.

There are about 10,000 of these South American Indians scattered over the San Blas Archipelago. They live almost independently of the Panamanian government and have their own regulations and laws. They survive mainly on the money gained from selling coconuts and each island, of which there are hundreds, is covered in coconut trees. The guide books told us that each tree is owned by someone and that they are all watched particularly when boats like ours arrived. The Kuna's other main trade is fishing for crustaceans and tuna, which are abundant in these areas. Simon and myself stood beside the largest of these Indians in the village and he only came up to our elbows. The village was a bizarre place. It was about the size of a football pitch and had nearly 2,000 people living in it. We arranged a tour with the local guide (the largest person on the island) and as we walked through the village it was strange that only the women seemed to wear the traditional clothes and not the men. The women's legs were bound with beads up to the knees and they wore brightly-coloured hand-painted skirts and tops. The men and, in particular, the boys all wore football jerseys or sports tops of some kind. We all found it amusing to see lots of Manchester United jerseys with Roy Keane written on the back.

As we walked Rebecca led the way and Simon was behind me. We rounded to the western side of the island and we could see the mainland jungle about five miles away. We came upon an old man who was sitting on a small stool, outside his hut, smoking a short pipe. His skin was very weathered and dark, almost leathery, and his feet although small were splayed wide by years of not wearing shoes. He beckoned us over to sit with him with a smile and to our surprise spoke English very well. We sat there and talked for a while, the three of us listening to him as he told us how things had changed since he was young and how the future of his people was very much in danger.

'When I was younger there were much fewer of us, only the stronger ones survived and there was enough for all of us, there were enough lobsters and fish to feed us, there was enough water to drink and the profit from the coconuts was sufficient to buy anything else we might have needed. Now there are too many, with medicines and doctors even the weak are surviving and we cannot continue much longer, everything is running out, and there isn't enough to go around.'

We left the old man after a while and the three of us were a little saddened by his comments. Progress for him spelled the end of his people. As we walked on we could sense that this beautiful small island wasn't going to be like this for very much longer. Soon the hotels, that have sprung up throughout the Caribbean, will come here, and like everywhere else these proud Indians will end up working in these resorts.

There were a few other boats anchored in Porvenir, the main island of the group, including a small American boat,

Madjk. Mike and Amy were husband and wife and they had three small kids, Danni, Jaye, and Keegan. Mike had come over and asked if I could give him a hand with fixing something on his mast and when Mike was up the mast Keegan sat down next to me on the deck. He was only five and had a worried look on his face as he looked at his Dad high up the rigging. I asked him what was wrong and he said that his Dad was going to get burned by the sun up there so high. I tried to reassure him that his Dad would be all right and that he wasn't going to stay up there too long but I don't think he was too sure. He was relieved when Mike returned to the deck. They were a great family and were like us travelling around the world, although they were going to take a little longer than us. Amy explained that the kids were doing their schoolwork by correspondence and they mailed back the assignments to the United States. Each morning on the boat the children did their schoolwork and in the afternoons were free to do what they wanted. It seemed like a fantastic experience for them but one that they probably wouldn't appreciate until they were much older. We went snorkelling with the children and had the whole family over for dinner – Tony treated the kids to some brownies.

Holger Danske arrived into Porvenir two days before we were due to head off. They had sailed from Aruba, the Dutch island, north of Venezuela. It was good to see Eric again. We invited him and his new crew over for dinner. Luckily we had caught a big tuna that day so there would be enough for us and his crew.

Before dinner Simon had one of the most frustrating phonecalls ever when he tried to call home from the one payphone on the island. We couldn't get any coins, we could not buy a call card because they didn't have any at the tiny bar, and couldn't reverse the charges or use a credit card because the operator refused. Simon politely asked her was there any way of making

a call to which she politely answered no and hung up, much to Simon's annoyance. We would have to wait until we got back to some sort of modern civilisation. I needed to buy him a beer, at the small corrugated iron shed bar on the beach, to cool him off.

Eric had a completely new crew since the last time we had met him. Anne was his first mate; she was an Australian and about thirty-five. Christine was a Dutch girl about twenty-four, and James a German of about the same age. We could sense that they were having crew problems from the moment we met them. Eric, while being very kind and decent to us, was I imagine a tough task-master. It did not surprise us that both James and Christine decided the following day to leave the boat and get on a flight to Panama city. Crew problems were something we were encountering all the time. We had met boats with crews who had begun the journey as the best of friends and after some time together on a boat turned out to be barely speaking to each other. The stresses of living together in a small space were often too much. We considered ourselves very lucky only to have family members on our boat. We had grown up together and knew each other's strengths and weaknesses and while we were finding out new things all the time we were starting out with a very intimate relationship.

Eric was in a bit of fix now with only himself and Anne to bring the boat to the canal from the San Blas islands and he asked if one of us would mind sailing the seventy miles or so with him. Rebecca decided she would do it, she got on pretty well with Anne and felt it would be okay for just one day. It felt a little strange for us to be one crew member down for the first time. We said our farewells to the crew of *Madjk,* and *Holger Danske* and ourselves raced the whole day – north to the canal.

The entrance to the port of Cristobal is between two huge breakwaters. We felt tiny in our boat trying to avoid the mas-

sive tankers that were everywhere. It is one of the great crossroads of the oceans and there were ships of all kinds. We made our way through the traffic being directed over the radio by the port authorities, much like planes are at an airport, to Cristobal Yacht Club in Colon. Colon is one of those rare places whose name aptly describes it. It is regarded as one of the most dangerous and violent cities in the world so we were a little apprehensive about arriving. Our fears were confirmed by the first person I met as we tied up to the dock. We had met Peter back in Grenada and as he helped us with our lines he told me that the previous night there had been a hold up at the bar in the yacht club. The two barmen had been badly beaten and the cash had been robbed. Everyone had been held at gun-point while their pockets were searched and everything taken.

It was in Colon, for the first time ever, I got a letter from my Dad. I was surprised that he would have taken the time to send me an epic letter. The two of us had grown quite close over the year before we left on the voyage, as I was living with him in Dublin. He was there two or three nights a week and we used to go out to dinner quite a bit. I can remember one night, in particular, at the beginning of our planning as the two of us sat at the bar in the Unicorn restaurant on Baggot Street. I was writing down the places on a piece of paper, a small piece of paper – the kind you would have stuffed in your wallet with someone's number written on it – Spain, Canary Islands, Caribbean, Panama, South Pacific Islands, Australia, Indonesia, Thailand, Sri Lanka, Red Sea. As Dad and I discussed the various stops and the timing of each one with regard to weather conditions, the barman wondered what in God's name were we talking about. I told him we were going to sail around the world and that these were the stops. I think he thought the two of us were crazy. It was the first time that I actually believed it was going to happen. In our family we had talked about these

sort of things often and the idea of a long voyage on the boat had nearly happened before but somehow hadn't work out and the idea fizzled away. This time it seemed different and Dad was tremendously excited about it. We had worked together all summer on the planning of the whole Sail Chernobyl project and while we argued a lot over the details we had worked well together. I laughed as I remembered one incident when I made him angry – I deliberately made him late for a meeting we were both going to. In his letter he joked about all those fights we had and he said he actually missed those times.

The transit through the Panama Canal was one of the highlights of the whole voyage. The canal is 50 miles long and was cut through one of the narrowest and lowest saddles of the long, mountainous isthmus that joins the North and South American continents. In 1534, Charles of Spain ordered the first survey of the proposed canal route, but it wasn't until three centuries later that the first construction began. The French laboured for 20 years, beginning in 1880, but disease and financial problems defeated them. In 1903 Panama and the United States signed a treaty under which the US undertook to construct the canal and bought the rights and properties from the failed French Canal Company. Like the Grand Canal in Dublin the Panama Canal consists of a series of locks that effectively act as steps that at first lead up from the Atlantic side to the giant man-made Gatun lake in the middle and then down again to the Pacific. There are two channels through each series of locks much like a dual-carriageway. As we approached the entrance it was a fantastic sight to see a massive container ship being lifted up in the lock some 85 feet above us. We, in our small sailing boat, were more of an annoyance than anything else to the canal operators. In the first lock we were behind a cruise ship called the *Victoria*. As the water began to rise we could hear, on the intercom of the ship, the captain explaining

what Sail Chernobyl was all about. We had no idea how he had found out about us but it was a great surprise when all the people on the ship came back to look down at us and wave.

The transit took two days and both *Holger Danske* and *Golden Apple* got through unscathed and without being run over by one of the massive ships. It was a wonderful day for us and one of the great turning points of the trip. Passing out of the last lock into the Pacific was like going into a whole new frontier. Rebecca and Tony stood on the bow and fought over who was going to be the first of us into the new ocean. We passed under the huge Bridge of the Americas that joins these two giant continents and made our way to Balboa Yacht Club on the edge of Panama city.

People who sail on their own are often some of the most interesting people you will meet and many of these loners tend to congregate in Panama. The bars in the yacht clubs at either side of the canal are great places to hear tales of travel and of woe.

Neil was from Schull, a small town in West Cork. Andy and I were sitting at the bar when we heard this thick West Cork accent. Neil had been travelling on his own for three years in a small boat that he had built himself, having previously working on cargo ships all over the world. *Beautiful Girl* was his second boat; his first had been wrecked on a reef back in the Los Roques Islands where we had been a few weeks earlier. Neil looked as much like a pirate as you could imagine, with big side burns and wild white hair and a decent size gut, Andy and I were almost expecting him to have a parrot on his soldier. He told us a story from Schull back in the 1960s when he was a young lad in his late teens: 'All the fishing boats in those days were small and there was no such thing as toilets or anything comfortable like you have on boats nowadays, you did your business in a barrel on the aft deck and that

was it and you washed in a bucket of cold sea water. A friend of my father's decided he wanted to get a decent sized boat that could stay out longer and go a bit further offshore. He decided to get the boat from Norway as that's where real boats were made he thought. When the boat arrived it was all kitted out with a proper galley and toilets and everything. But there was lots of pornography on the inside walls. You know the way those Scandinavians are about that stuff. The boat had to be blessed by the priest before being put to sea, so the lads thought they better rip out all the panelling with the posters of the naked women before the priest came to give the blessing. When the priest came he wondered what all the mess was about and one of the lads told him about the porno. He laughed and said there was no need to go to all that trouble and ruin a good boat on account of him coming to bless her, sure what was the harm in a few pictures.'

Neil went on with these stories all night, half of them made up and half true, I think he was delighted to have a couple of willing Irish ears. He seemed to be a lonely soul and I wonder where he is now.

Another man, an American called Dick, had a sad tale. Having retired from the United States navy ten years previously he and his wife had decided they wanted to spend the rest of their years sailing around the world, and set about building a boat themselves. A few months before they were due to depart from Florida she was diagnosed with cancer and died only weeks later. He had left on his own and confessed to me that he really didn't know where he was going and that he was terribly lonely. We were to meet many more of these lone sailors as we progressed across the Pacific, most of them tempted by the beautiful and peaceful islands, places where they could forget their pasts and forge a new travelling life with no ties. For us it was a real eye-opener to meet such a

diverse range of people from the multi-millionaire super-yacht owner to the lone sailor.

Panama city was, much more than Venezuela, as I had imagined South America to be – hot, sleazy and exciting. The city bustled with energy and colour; the buses were all old and highly decorated with lights and artistic graffiti. The streets were packed with cars and the sound of blaring horns was almost deafening. Everyone seemed to be shouting and screaming at each other. We went to the cinema for the first time since we left to see the blockbuster *Titanic* – a rather odd choice you might think considering what we were doing. We were all a little disappointed at the film as we thought it seemed to miss the point of one of the greatest tragedies and focused on a love affair.

We did a massive shop in the big supermarkets in the city to fully stock up the boat. Panama was a very cheap place and would be one of the last places where we would find decent shops until we arrived in Australia on the other side of the Pacific. Andy and Tony arrived back to the boat with over thirty boxes, everything from canned beans to shampoo. It was difficult to plan what we would need so far in advance but Tony at this stage had become a real expert in provisioning the boat so we trusted him completely. Simon, Bec and I headed off to get more spares for the boat, engine oils, light bulbs and various other things that we knew would be difficult to get for a long time.

I didn't really get a chance to see that much of Panama city as I spent most of the time trying to catch up on my writing. As I said earlier I had promised Dad that I would send him a few chapters before we headed off into the Pacific. I was working right up until we departed and was relieved to have managed to get something off to him.

We were all excited about our next stop – the Galapagos

Islands. We passed out through the harbour slowly on the evening of 7 March with Eric and his new crew behind us. We caught a glimpse of a giant American nuclear submarine. Its sinister looking black hull slid under as the sun set behind the skyscrapers of Panama city.

The moon was huge; the sea calm but for the gentle roll that there always is in a great ocean. The face of the moon rolled with the water, gently rippling with the gusts that quietly whispered across the surface. These gusts are what we longed for, as each one brushed the sails it pushed us forward. It is a beautiful feeling to be pushed like this on a still night, almost magical. It's these nights that make the rough ones seem worthwhile, nature seems at peace. I could never sleep when nature chose, so rarely, to combine her full pale face with a cloudless sky and a calm sea – too perfect to be wasted by ordinary dreams. We whispered and moved slowly, careful not disturb this harmony and the only real sound was the waves and the wake that followed, glistening with phosphorescence, like little stars shaking and weaving in their own small whirlpools as they are disturbed by the rudder. We were still next to Eric after the 1,000 miles or so since Panama. It was amazing that we had never been out of sight of each other. I think they were enjoying the night like us, we could see the silhouettes of their heads in the cockpit.

St Cristobal arose from the horizon with the day, 12 March, her bright green lushness flooded in the warm equatorial sun. The cliffs that form the island's frontier to the ocean are huge and black, formed during violent underwater eruptions. St Cristobal and the other islands in the archipelago are the tips of huge submarine volcanoes that sit on what is called the Galapagos platform – an underwater range whose peaks form islands that breathe above the Pacific some 1,000 miles west of Panama. Charles Darwin made these islands famous, as it was

here that he formed the basis for his origin of the species theory. These mystical islands of giant tortoises, marine iguanas and the blue-footed booby, are where our links to the animal kingdom were confirmed some 150 years ago. It had an enchantment for me that can only be described as an expectation of something unique and unspoiled, a harmony borne of nature's greatness, a showcase.

Ironically the first sign of life we met was in the form of death. A seal floated on the water, dead and bloated, swollen almost to the point of bursting, her black coat bleached from the sun and dirtied with sea grass. We passed her on our port side before we came to the reef that broke on the point on the northern side of Wreck Bay. The swell curled around the corner before breaking white on the coral in the early morning sun. We anchored on the northern shore of the bay near a little beach, where local children were swimming and playing football.

We were glad to be in, we had left bustling Panama a week before and all of us were tired. There had been very little wind and the sun had burned us all. On one of the really hot days Tony and I had spent about two hours sitting in the shade of the sails, in nothing but shorts, pouring buckets of sea water over ourselves in an effort to cool down. The calmness had been strange. We were in the biggest ocean in the world and not a ripple but for the occasional rain shower. Each evening the sunset had flooded the sea, oranges, reds and pinks combining to create an unreal image much like cheap department store art. The horizon circled us, unbroken, nothing in the way. We were always the centre of an infinite circle of empty sea. If you had been in a plane above us you probably wouldn't have seen us but if you did we would have looked like two specks of dust in a giant dark blue puddle.

There were seals all along the shore, everywhere we

turned they were sleeping, their soft blubbery bodies awkward on the land. The pier was covered with them and as we landed in our dinghy they barked and stood up proud with their whiskered noses up and eyes blinking. They watched us as we climbed up the steps, their heads still, much like a curious dog would be with strangers approaching. They smell, they smell of the sea, of fish and the smell hung along the shore like a curtain, not unpleasant but strong. Behind lay the town. Puerto Baquerizo Moreno was much bigger than we had anticipated. The buildings were low-lying and beige, curling around the inlet in a crescent and a small river came down from the hills behind. There was an army barracks next to the pier and beside the pier was a small beach. The guards were dressed impeccably in all white, not a stain on their proud uniforms, their boots a shiny black like their hair, and moustaches on their tanned Spanish-looking faces. They nodded stiffly as we passed on our way into the town.

Looking back now everything was perfect in those first few days in Galapagos, a land that is brimming with life. We toured the island searching out the unique wild-life and found the black marine iguanas that looked baked, almost carbonised, under the hot sun, their faces like something from a time when dinosaurs were common. The seals were everywhere, they would sleep in the dinghy when we left it on the beach and they would wobble away annoyed when we returned. There were many trails through the rocks that led up to the cliffs and the view was breathtaking. We all stood for hours on the man-made platform that was like a human nest perched over the bay. The great albatross soared overhead effortlessly gliding on the uplifts and gusts that blew in our faces, the giant billed pelicans dived for the unsuspecting little fish swimming near the surface. Under this aerial show the seals lay basking on the rocks occasionally being cooled by a wave that managed to

spill over them. They would flap their fins at the sudden cooling and quickly resume their motionless snoozing. A blue-footed booby stood on the cliff near us, and looked at us inquisitively, these birds with their blue feet and narrow eyes look somewhat stupid, but then again we probably looked just as stupid to him. Andrew tried diligently to capture all this with the video camera, which in itself was quite amusing. It was as if the birds were playing with him, speeding up and diving and soaring, while Andrew tried to follow their flight. With his right eye glued to the view finder he was going around in a dizzy spin and almost fell over a few times. Those few days for me were the highlight of the voyage. It was a place where I felt lucky to be and where anyone would feel lucky to be alive, where what is good on this earth combines into a feast of life and where I could stand and watch and be amazed by nature's charm and diversity.

Then we heard that he had died.

◊

It was 14 March at about seven in the morning local time when we heard that something serious had happened at home. Luckily we were all up early as we were supposed to be going diving that morning with hammerhead sharks. Email had become our means of communicating with the outside world and when we saw the little yellow light flashing by the chart table we knew there was a message. Receiving messages had been a great novelty and we all looked forward to them enormously, it was our only link with our friends and family. There were actually two messages that morning both very short and both telling us that we should contact home immediately. It's difficult to describe how we felt, we knew something was up but didn't really have any idea about what could have happened. The only clue I suppose at that stage was that it wasn't Dad

who had sent the message. Normally if there had ever been a crisis at home it would be he who would contact us, this time it was Patrick our older brother. Simon, Andrew and myself headed in to the shore to find a phone.

I can still see Simon's face wince as he took in what Patrick said to him. He nodded his head and his voice cracked a little as his eyes flooded. It was obvious something as terrible as we had been trying not to imagine had happened. Our father had died in an awful accident. The three of us were dazed like someone had punched us hard in the gut; the tears slowly trickled from each of us. Nothing can prepare you for suddenly losing someone who means more than anything or anybody. All of a sudden there is just a giant hole, which no matter what you try to do just seems to get bigger and deeper. The contrast could not have been greater, in a place that is so brimming with life of all kinds, from the beautiful frigate birds so effortlessly flying above the water to the giant tortoises plodding over the rough grass. All I will remember of the Galapagos is the giant wound that was carved so suddenly out of me while I was there. Perhaps that dead seal was an omen.

We left the telephone exchange and walked through the empty Sunday morning streets back to the quay. We slowly went back out to the boat. None of us could really say anything; Rebecca and Tony were waiting on the deck. Tears rolled down Rebecca's cheeks as we approached, we didn't really have to say anything, they both knew something awful had happened by our faces. Simon told them. The bay was still, Wreck Bay, St Cristobal had torn us apart and for the first time since we had left Ireland there was a complete sense of despair.

Eric was a tremendous comfort to us that morning, he helped us re-anchor the boat and arrange the flight to mainland South America where we would connect on towards home.

We flew over our beloved *Golden Apple* two hours later. I

could see her bobbing in the bay, the Sail Chernobyl flags still flying. It all seemed over, I felt we might never see her again, and sitting on that plane I thought about the months we had spent getting this far.

It wasn't until we got to New York that any of us really believed all this was real. It was in JFK that we first met Irish people who offered their condolences. As we waited in the lounge for the flight to Shannon we caught our first look at some of the Irish newspapers. All the papers carried the story and as we read the grim details of the search on the cliffs and in the sea it was hard to believe that it was our father. It was like reading about someone else.

6

All Changed

Seeing the dead man lie there in a box surrounded by flowers, I didn't see my father. The only part of him that I recognised was his hands. They were crossed on his chest over his gold and navy tie. They were big the way I always remembered them, the veins were still there only the blood didn't move, they looked real and they looked his. His face was covered in make-up and looked plastic and fake, the collar of his shirt was too big for his now deflated neck. The shirt looked too stiff but at least they tied his top button, he really hated not having his top button closed and used, when we were small, always close ours. Just one of those stupid things. The make-up couldn't cover the cuts on his lips and right ear, they were real and at least they showed that he was human and gave some clue as to why he was here, in this box in this awful room.

Looking at him there I wondered how he must have felt as he fell and how scared he must have been, clambering on the rocks. It's difficult for me to picture him so helpless so alone and so frightened. I try to picture it in my head but I can't, I had never seen him frightened and certainly never so helpless. For me he was bullet-proof. What was he thinking at that moment, the moment when he knew he was in trouble? Hopefully he was unconscious at this stage so he didn't really know that he would die, hopefully he just hit his head and that was it, hopefully he didn't have time to think knowing those would be his last thoughts. He would have hated to evaluate his own life even if only for a second or two. He hated to look back on things whether good or bad, and he was always very bad at talking about himself, so I suppose thinking about himself or

his own life would have been just as difficult for him. Hopefully he didn't gasp for air as he went down. The lonely silence as the water took him and filled him and surrounded him in a suffocating grip and then the silence as he floated to the bottom and lay there motionless suspended in the icy water below the waves. I cried as I thought of him there, so alone and so quiet.

As I see him lying here before me I realise I will never know any of these things, those thoughts are gone like the rest of him, and what do I have left? For some people the memory of how a person was like is often better than they actually were, we tend to remember only what we choose. But for me, at that moment, memories are useless and so pathetically inadequate that I don't want them, not now anyway. I want to leave and I wish they would close the lid on the coffin, I really don't want anyone else seeing him like this and he would have hated it as well.

Mum was in the car with her mother. As we passed we couldn't believe it was her. We pulled in and ran to her. Her knees crumbled when she saw us there on the side of the road. We held her up, all of us with tears in our eyes. She was frightened and couldn't really say anything she just held on to us tightly relieved we were home, she said to Simon, 'you brought them home to me, I'm so glad you're all here.' We stay there embracing for a minute or so. It's now it all becomes so real, I can see and feel the pain she is going through, her heart broken and ripped apart in such an unfair way, a sudden loneliness that she can't really understand. I can only imagine what the previous two days had been like for her, the waiting, the searching, desperate hope, and despair and then the truth. She was like a frightened little girl; pale and drawn, her eyes were glazed in disbelief that all this was happening to her.

When we got home I wanted to go down to the cliff where he had fallen, I knew Simon would go with me. It really is a

beautiful place, he loved it more than anywhere else, he used to walk there any chance he got, he would stride out there onto the headland with the dogs in tow. He had a big stride and would hum to himself as he walked, like on Saturday mornings around the house he would hum when he made Mum's breakfast, diligently cutting the toast and cracking the top of the egg. It was always windy there, even if it was calm at home. The wheat had been sown and the green shoots had broken through the stony soil. It wasn't good farmland. He hadn't really bought it for farming, he and Mum were going to retire there and spend their days looking out to sea and talking and taking stock of all they had achieved together. That time in one's life when marriage becomes real again, like it was at the beginning, just two to talk and listen. The view was breathtaking and the sea was calm. We slowly walked down to the edge. It had never appeared that dangerous to me before but now I was more cautious. The two of us sat there and looked over, down on the rocks below, and wondered what could have happened to him. We tried to piece together what could have happened, we didn't really know the facts or why he was there, but we tried nonetheless to figure out how he could have died here in a place he knew so well. We stayed there for an hour or so.

◊

We were seated in the front row as is normal at removals, I hate them, I have always hated this Irish ritual of death, publicly prolonging the agony, allowing people to come and see us upset, to try and look into the coffin. The coffin is shut thank God. I am standing next to Mum as the people begin to file past. Most people don't know what to say or do, and just fumble for words of condolence. The nuns are the experts and they say all the right holy things that are supposed to make you feel

better, they annoyed me a little and gave no comfort – how can their words possibly mean anything to me. I don't know most of the people and it becomes easy to let them say they are sorry for your trouble. It's the people that I know well are the ones who hurt me, they knew him and knew how much he meant to me. I was glad they came. Most of the time I am helping Mum, she knows most of the people, and each person for her is an individual reminder of him. There are people from all walks of life and thousands of them all coming to pay their respects. Patrick stops it after about two hours; we have all had enough. We carry the coffin out, the six sons, Mum and Rebecca follow. It's dark and I can see faces everywhere, it's drizzling and we are surrounded by people. It's a relief when we make it into the car; it is quiet and warm, at least for a few minutes until we reach the church.

The Blackrock church seems huge. Its high ceiling seems even higher than I remembered it and as we walk up the aisle carrying the coffin I can again just see lots of faces, sad faces watching us as we tread slowly on the cold floor. He feels heavier this time, I suppose it's just a longer walk. I wonder why all these people are here? In what way had he touched them that they felt the need to come? Was it something small or large, was it just because they admired him or something more tangible or was it just that they felt they should be there, any way there are hundreds of people. I try to imagine how he would have felt if he could have looked out of the coffin, what he would have said, how embarrassed he would have been by all this attention. I can remember him, only six months previously, at the funeral of his own mother, our grandmother. He was quiet and his eyes watered a little as he gave a faint smile when people approached him to offer their condolences. To be honest I wasn't very upset when my grandmother died, she had led a good and long life, but to see him upset made me feel

upset, he rarely showed us this side.

The people filed past again for a while but we didn't stay long. It was strange coming home that night. I wasn't tired despite how many people were telling me how tired I should be after flying across the world. Everyone was quiet and subdued which is a rare thing in our house where there is usually so much going on. As families go we always were an extremely lucky one. There had never really been any serious problems and all of us were happy, a little spoilt I suppose. When something has been so good for so long it is difficult to know how to react when it all goes wrong so suddenly. None of us was used to tragedy or real hardship. We had never really had to experience feelings like despair or extreme sadness because there had never really been a cause. I'm not saying that everything was perfect by any means but I don't think any of us would have wanted it any different. Now we were all a little lost. When everyone had gone to bed I stayed up for while on my own. It was a relief to be on my own, I had felt lonely in those crowds, I needed to think some of this through without the worry of keeping up appearances. I began to think about what had happened and quietly cry, not in a hysterical way, just sad, sad that something like this should happen to me and to us and to him.

We were all in the priest's house about a half an hour before the funeral mass was to begin. We were due to meet the President before we went across to the church. To be honest we were all kind of dreading it, Mum in particular. We had no idea what she was going to be like, whether she would be desperately official and cold or whether she would contrive an emotional concern. Mary McAleese arrived in the flagged car accompanied by an officer from the army. Simon, Patrick and I were standing outside the house, I was smoking and the lads were keeping me company. From the moment we started talking to

her I knew she was a cool woman. She said that she had met Mum and Dad years before when she was a young journalist and had wondered then why he would have ever wanted to go into politics. She was both very genuine and warm without losing the importance of her position. Mum, when she saw her asked, with her typical charm and warmth, if it was OK for her to hug the President, they both smiled and hugged. Mum said to me much later that she was very pleased to have met her and that contrary to what she thought beforehand, she actually got comfort from meeting her in those horrible circumstances.

It was quite overwhelming when we walked into the church. We walked slowly through the sacristy from behind the altar to the front row of seats. As I walked I kept my head down careful not to catch anyone's eyes. I did look up once and felt a shiver at the thousands of faces that were looking up at us, so many people care I thought, so many people have come.

Father George's sermon was a glowing tribute. About halfway through it Mum, who was sitting next to me, quietly, in between tears, smiled and said to me, 'he was no fecking saint you know'. That is typical of my mother, always so honest and straight even at a time like this. There are many things that I could say about my father but none would really do justice to the way we all both loved and respected him. Towards the end of the mass Patrick had asked Father George if he could say a few words and I think for us this was the hardest moment of all. I think Patrick summed up my father's greatest points better than anyone, how he managed to say these things at a time like this I shall never know. I shall always be amazed at how he coped with all the funeral arrangements on his own when we were so very far away. He is someone of tremendous strength and during these days I was incredibly proud to be his brother.

'My father liked a crowd. He would have wanted to speak to each of you. It may have taken some time but that would have been his style. We will not be able to do that today but I would like to express our sincere gratitude to all of you for coming. Many of you were integrally involved in the search for him last weekend while others have called, either by phone or in person, to comfort our family since then. We are very moved.

'He was a human dynamo. Anyone who ever shared a business meeting, canvassed a housing estate or raced a sailing boat with him will recognise the enthusiasm and boundless energy which so characterised my father. Not for him the comfort of a large party canvass, he wanted to personally visit every home, to converse with every person, to solve every problem. He lived his life at a hundred miles an hour and if anything seemed to accelerate with age.

'My father believed in giving. Not because he had to, but because he wanted to. He took joy, genuine joy in the service of others. And when he gave he gave in style. He had this unique ability to simultaneously see the big picture while at the same time immerse himself in all of the little details. He knew exactly what he wanted to build but was happiest piecing it together himself, inch by last inch.

'Finally, my father loved so very deeply. He loved Ireland. Not in an aggressive or nationalistic way, but rather out of a deep sense of affection for Ireland as a place, and for all of us as its people. Cork held a special place in his heart. Not just the city, where he worked for over 40 years and he served as a truly outstanding Councillor, Lord Mayor and Government Minister, but also the Tracton area where he lived and walked, and in which he chose to raise his family. He had enormous affection for the county of Cork and West Cork in particular, where he sailed extensively and where we as a family spent many happy summers.

'No expression of my father's love would be complete without mentioning his family. He was the perfect father, or at least as close to it as I have ever seen. I know he took enormous pleasure in all that we

did. To the crew of the Golden Apple *who were in the Pacific Ocean until Sunday morning, he was sponsor, mentor, coach, and so immensely proud. He spoke openly to me about how much he looked forward to seeing them round Roches Point in July 1999. I suspect it would have been his proudest moment. Simon and Rory, Andrew and Tony, Rebecca and David all remember him in different ways and those of you who know each of them will understand how they feel. To me Dad was not just my father but my closest friend. I will always regret that he was taken from me just as I finally felt able to reciprocate that friendship.*

'My mother was everything to him. Micheál Martin described them as the "Golden Couple" to me the other night and they were indeed that. They lit up Cork for nearly thirty years and had the most blissful, complete and wonderful marriage. Had he tried to put it in words I suspect he would have chosen Yeats. I hope that you will allow me to do so now:

> *Though I am old with wandering*
> *Through hollow lands and hilly lands*
> *I will find out where she has gone*
> *And kiss her lips and take her hands*
> *And walk among long dappled grass*
> *And pluck till time and times are done*
> *The silver apples of the moon*
> *The golden apples of the sun.'*

PATRICK COVENEY, 18 MARCH 1998

◊

That evening it was great to meet all my friends again. I wasn't sure if I wanted them to all come down to the house or not but once they were all there it was a great relief to hear all the laughs again. I hadn't seen most of them for months and it was great to catch up on all the news and tell them of my adventures. Even if only for a short while, I managed to forget why I was

home. Over the coming weeks our friends were absolutely fantastic to all of us. I don't think we had to cook a meal or wash an item of clothing, people just kept coming to help out. The cards of condolences came in their thousands, from so many different people several of whom we had never met, there were so numerous in fact that we found it difficult to get time to read all of them. We have them all, filed away, maybe some day I will go through them. The poor postman was completely snowed under.

Since we had arrived home there had been the constant question in each of our minds whether we would continue the voyage or remain at home. It became clear early on that one of us at least would have to stay on at home with Mum. We were not prepared to leave her on her own to cope with everything. Patrick had to go back to London where he was working and David although tremendous throughout all this was really too young to be of any real support to Mum in the months ahead. To be honest none of us were really ready to make any sort of decision so soon after all that had happened. But the reality was that the boat was sitting in Wreck Bay in the Galapagos Islands and had to be moved – we only had a permit to stay on there for another week. It was either going west if we were to continue or east if we were abandoning the project. After much thinking on our own and discussion among all of us a compromise solution was decided on. We would all stay at home for the next month or so and then four of us would return to finish the voyage. Simon was to stay at home and look after the farm and help out Mum. I was to become skipper.

In the meantime we organised to have friends of ours deliver the boat from the Galapagos to Tahiti in French Polynesia, so we could keep on schedule. The next few weeks were spent organising our return and we were all very industrious, almost as busy as we were before we left the first time. It was to be a

new beginning, a whole new start with a new crew.

I think for the four of us the trip took on a much greater significance, more of a mission than an adventure. The whole project had been as much a dream of Dad's as ours and there was no way we were going to let him down, and end the voyage. We had also made a commitment to Adi Roche and her team. In a gesture of great selflessness Mum gave us her blessing. She told me that Dad had said to her many times that to see his children bring *Golden Apple* past Roches Point, having sailed around the world, would be one of his proudest moments. She wanted us to finish. The last thing Patrick said to me before we headed off was that we had all become a little more precious now, so just be extra careful. And so on 8 May we headed off to the other side of the world to resume our voyage. There were not many people at the airport to see us off, but Dad's best friend stood by the security check at Cork airport. He had searched all night like a true hero for my father and it was he who had found little Sasha barking on the rocks early that Sunday morning.

He didn't really have to say anything, he just wished us luck.

7

New Beginnings

Coming back to the boat I did feel a little apprehensive. We had been so busy before we left that like the first time we hadn't really had time to think about what was in store for us. My role on the boat up until now had been relatively undefined. Simon was the skipper, Andrew was the navigator, and Tony was the cook. Rebecca and I were crew members each with specialities, hers being medical and mine was with computers. I had also, given that I was the only one who had been to Belarus, been the expert on the work of the charity we were helping and did many of the interviews and presswork. It had been a system that had worked very well; it was a team with complementary skills, with each person doing what they did best. Morale on a boat is more important that anything else. In such a small place the key role for any leader is to try to ensure that everyone is happy as well as pulling his or her weight. Simon's strength as skipper had been his great optimism and good nature. This was something that was going to be of great importance as we recommenced the trip particularly after our family tragedy.

Apart from the crew dynamics, I knew I was going to miss Simon as a friend and brother. Simon and I hadn't always been the best of friends, we were and are very different but we had grown very close over the previous few months. We were all going to miss him but I think maybe me a little bit more than the others.

So much had changed and so suddenly that it was difficult to get a grip on it all. I knew we would be working very much as a team but it was my ultimate responsibility to get the boat home. Full responsibility was not something I was used to and

I was now in charge. The trip had taken on an even greater profile – having decided to finish what we had started had generated fantastic support at home in both the fundraising drive and personal admiration from friends. We had to finish.

We were lucky to be arriving back to *Golden Apple* in one of the most beautiful parts of the world. After about a week in the harbour in Papeete in Tahiti we set off to explore this wonderful paradise. The week had been a busy one with much to be done on the boat. Andrew and Tony hauled out the sewing machine and set about repairing the sails, Rebecca began cleaning the upholstery and I was stuck down in the engine room doing the necessary oil and filter changes. We also installed the satellite telephone that we had brought from Ireland so we would be able to have normal telephone calls to and from the boat no matter where we were, whether out in the middle of the ocean or in port. The main reason for this was so that Mum could call us whenever she felt worried about us and it also turned out to be great for keeping in touch with the media in Ireland. In some ways it took from the adventure a little bit knowing that we were only a telephone call away from anyone, but it did make practical sense.

Ted was with us for the week. He was one of the crew who delivered the boat, some 4,000 miles, from the Galapagos to Tahiti. He had kindly agreed to stay on and mind the boat for an extra week until we arrived. Ted looked like he had been at sea for years. He was very thin and his skin had gone a deep brown in the hot tropical sun. His face was very wrinkled, his beard was very overgrown and he smoked. The white smoke puffed through the grey beard. His shirt was blue but faded like his eyes. He had a big mole over his left eye and it was partly covered by his sandy grey hair that like his beard was overgrown – your regular captain Bird's Eye. We had known him for years, he had helped out Patrick and Andrew when

they used to sail dinghies and he was the first person we talked to when we arrived that night in Tahiti. We were glad to see him and to see that the boat was in one piece. He told us about their voyage and what had broken and what was away being repaired and gave us lists of what was left of our stores. We were lonely seeing *Golden Apple* again after all that happened. I think each of us privately thought how sad it was that Dad would never see his beautiful boat again.

Eric was also in Papeete harbour and it was good to see a familiar face. He was anxious to know how we all were and how things had been at home. He was leaving before us and we agreed to meet up with him in Raiatea one of the western islands near Bora Bora.

Our first stop upon leaving Papeete was Moorea. This beautiful island, about twenty miles north of Tahiti, was just as I had imagined the South Pacific to be. The mountains were very high and almost came straight out of the sea and below them was a ring of rain forest so lush and dense it was difficult to see through it. We were anchored at the top of Cook Bay, which is like a fjord that cuts right into the island. It was amazing to sit on the deck and look up at the steep mountains that towered just behind us. It was the most beautiful anchorage we had been in so far. The beauty however was lost on Andy and myself as we both got a heavy dose of food poisoning. Although Tony denied it, it must have been something he cooked. I had a rather embarrassing experience the following day of getting a dose of diarrhoea as I was hoisting the mainsail. No one seemed to know what was going on when I called out from the mast asking someone else to take over. They did find it funny to see me somewhat shamefully hobble down below to the toilet.

Peter and Melanie were Eric's new crew. They were going to take Eric's boat from French Polynesia to Australia. He had

decided that he wasn't going to continue the voyage, I think his wife was anxious that he return to Sydney where they were building their new home. Peter and Melanie were both from Sydney. They were young and it was great to have a few like-minded people around as we hadn't really met other young people since we came back. We were delighted they would be coming at least as far as Fiji and as we left for Bora Bora we agreed that we would meet up again. We said our farewells to Eric. He had been with us since Las Palmas and we were a little sad to be leaving him. He had been there with us in the Galapagos when everything had gone so horribly wrong and had been great to us. He was off to Sydney and more than likely we would never see him again. A feature of the trip that each of us found difficult is that most of the people we met we would never see again.

Bora Bora is described by many as being the most beautiful island in the world and it probably is. The island has a massive dark green peak and the lush rain forests overhang golden sands that lead to gardens of coral so beautiful that they almost seem heavenly. The colours if you were to paint them would seem incongruous and unnatural, but here colour is everything, the turquoise water darkens as the coral rises in mounds of pinks, blues, greens, yellows. Around this kaleidoscope of brightness swim the most beautiful fish you could ever see, thousands of them all sizes, shapes, stripes, spots and colours. Below the crustaceans bustle and crawl and the giant clams yawn as their bright blue lips sieve the passing plankton. The people echo this colour and beauty. Both sexes have unblemished skin and dress as brightly as their wonderful environment and seem to have a perpetual air of happiness. We stayed here for a few days before heading off towards Tonga.

Since coming back to *Golden Apple* Andy and myself had not really been seeing eye to eye. I knew he found it difficult

with me being the skipper. Andrew was by far the most accomplished sailor of all of us, including Simon. He had navigated a number of boats before this trip and had raced a number of boats successfully. It had been different when Simon was there as Simon had been much older and as you might know most friction in families happens between siblings who are closest in age. It was also taking me some time to get used to my new responsibilities. I had been somewhat indecisive not about major things but small things like where we should anchor or who should do the various chores. Every decision was becoming an argument between us and it was putting all of us on edge. I decided that we had better thrash it out and we did and, I think, from then on things seemed to improve. I needed to change and learn much more about navigation and he agreed to cool down a bit and give me a chance.

The whales were truly amazing. As we sailed towards the northern islands of Tonga we were surrounded by six Minke whales. Each of them was the size of the boat and as they surfaced in the waves next to us they appeared to be playing and surfing. One flipped completely out of the water and we could see the full size of the creature before it crashed back into the waves. They were intrigued with us and we could see clearly that their big eyes were watching us as they cruised by the bow and passed us. They stayed for over an hour and we were fascinated to watch such big animals so in control and at one with their environment. By comparison we seemed so clumsy. They could glide through the water much like birds do in the sky, but we needed sails or an engine to move. I don't mean to be getting philosophical but it did seem that in certain domains we as human beings were almost pathetic. While we can strive to manage we can never really compete with such effortless grace. I found the beauty of such elegance most humbling.

With the exception of seeing the whales it had been a fairly

uneventful crossing from French Polynesia to Tonga. Our auto-pilot system had once again broken so we had to have some-one steering all the time. After a week this became very tiring particularly as it had been quite rough. We were doing watches at night with two people in an effort to break up the amount of time spent steering. With the reduced crew it meant three hours on deck and three hours in bed usually starting after dinner at around eight o'clock and finishing the following morning. It was strange getting so little sleep but what was stranger was constantly being woken in the middle of dreams. People dream every night but for the most part don't remember very much. We would always remember our dreams being woken in the middle of them and they became a real topic of conversation during the day, when each of us would recount our sleeping adventures. Psychologists who have researched sleep patterns say that constant sleep disruption over long periods of time can drive people crazy, I don't know if it's true but at times we did all get a little crazy. Our moods would change quite a lot but never for very long, the important thing was to try to leave each other alone when we were feeling down.

We crossed the International Date Line, which is just east of Tonga sometime on 3 June, so 4 June didn't exist for us this year – we had lost a day in one day if you know what I mean. We would of course gain it back over the next few months. We were now twelve hours ahead of time in Ireland instead of being twelve hours behind. Tongans say their country is the land where time begins because it's the first country just west of the dateline.

We arrived in Vava'u, the northern province of the king-dom of Tonga on the night of the Friday, 5 June. It was beauti-ful much like our arrival in the Galapagos. The steep cliffs glow-ed silvery in the moonlight as we navigated our way through the fringing islands and surrounding reefs into the safe haven

of Neifu harbour. We were lucky that there was a ship in front of us, which helped show us the way. Once again the phosphorescence bubbled and rolled, this time clearly visible in the wake from the ship's propeller. We had charts of the area, but it was much easier having the ship in front of us entering the harbour. We were fortunate to find an adequate mooring to which we tied up for the night. Peter and Melanie in *Holger Danske* had arrived before us and they came over for a beer to welcome us in. We all enjoyed a wonderful night's sleep.

The following morning we were confronted by immigration, customs, quarantine and the port authorities all at once. They boarded together and carried out their usual inspections and paper work. They were an amusing group, all big and fat, and after their initial formal demeanour were very friendly. They, like most of the officials in third world countries, insisted on stamping everything, passports, immigration forms, boat documents, etc. It's astounding how many forms I had to fill out – a process that would take several hours if not a whole day. The important thing is not to become in any way agitated with these people because it only makes the whole process take longer. Officials everywhere found it incredible that the skipper of a boat was so young. In fact everyone we met found it astonishing. Most of the crews of boats sailing around the world are made up of retired couples, who more often than not have sold up everything to buy a boat. So we were unique – four young people from the same family.

We only stayed in Tonga for the weekend and it was a truly wonderful stop-over on our way to meet Mum and David in Fiji. It was a poor place but it was here that for the first time I met people who seemed incredibly content and happy with what they had and how their life was. On the Saturday evening we went, with Peter and Melanie, to a local Tongan feast and while this was very much a touristy sort of thing to

do it did give a wonderful flavour of the Tongan way of life and culture. It was on a beach and included local music and dancing, eating and drinking. Local children wearing some magnificently coloured outfits put on a wonderful dancing performance even though many of them were shy and very young. Afterwards we enjoyed some kava – a local narcotic drink made from the kava root that is crushed into a powder and added to water. It takes quite a few cups to have any effect but soon my tongue went sort of numb and it was a good feeling despite kava tasting like dishwater. We then sat on the ground surrounded by local dishes. These included various types of fish including octopus, breadfruit, pineapple, watermelon, aubergines and some other unknown vegetables. Rebecca went berserk at one stage when a big lizard ran over her leg.

After dinner we stayed on talking to Matoto our host and his musicians. Matoto was old and weathered and had lived on these islands all his life. He explained to me how he had once been to Nuku'alofa the capital of Tonga and how the pace of life there and the relative unfriendliness of the people scared him and that he couldn't wait to get back to the islands of the north. The two musicians were great characters. The banjo player had a funny habit of holding his cigarette between his toes while he sat on the ground and strummed. Melanie broke into song. She had been in a band when she was in school and had a good voice.

After the feast we headed for the only night-club in the town of Neifu. Apart from their good nature the most overwhelming characteristic of Tongans is their size. Almost without exception they are all huge both in height and girth, male and female. The sight of over a hundred giant people gyrating to pop tunes is stunning. The women also have the habit of punching the men, as a form of flirting which everyone seems

Child in No. 1 Orphanage, Minsk

Adi Roche and the children from Chernobyl on the boat before we head off to sea [photo: John Sheehan]

The Coveneys in October 1997 launching the project in Dublin – from left – Simon, Hugh, Rory, Pauline, Tony, Rebecca, Andrew and David in front [photo: John Sheehan]

Heading out to sea from Cork harbour [photo: John Sheehan]

All the ARC boats in Las Palmas [photo: Andrew Coveney]

Andrew checking everything is OK with the mast [photo: Rory Coveney]

Pauline painting our logo on the wall in Las Palmas [photo: Rory Coveney]

Dave getting a transatlantic tow – no sharks around! [photo: Rory Coveney]

Arriving into St Lucia – land at last! [photo: Rory Coveney]

Dave, Rebecca and Andrew enjoying their Christmas dinner in Martinique

Pauline and Hugh in Palm Island [photo: Rory Coveney]

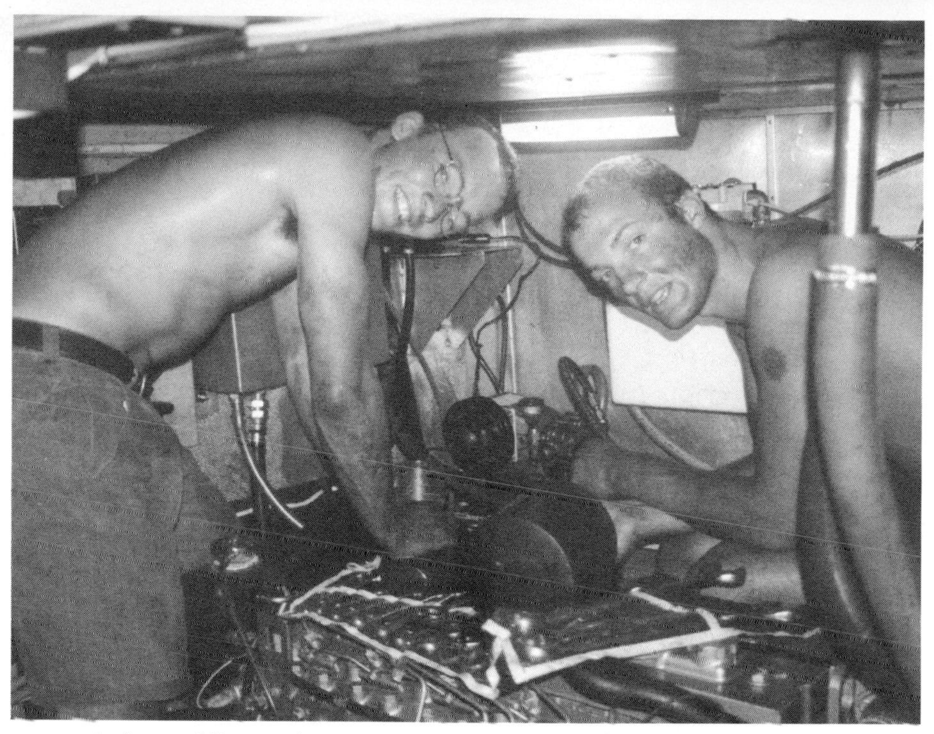

Andrew and Rory getting greasy in the engine room [photo: Rebecca Coveney]

Andrew looking happy with a big tuna [photo: Rory Coveney]

Going through the Panama Canal – from left – Tony, Rory, Simon, Rebecca and Andrew [photo: Anne Cleghorn]

Rebecca and Andrew want to be the first into the Pacific Ocean [photo: Rory Coveney]

Simon inspecting the local wildlife in Galapagos [photo: Rory Coveney]

Little Keegan with his big ears! [photo: Rory Coveney]

Golden Apple *safely anchored in Tonga* [photo: Andrew Coveney]

Friendly locals in Somosomo, Fiji [photo: Rory Coveney]

Andrew, with Rebecca, plotting our journey at the chart table [photo: Rory Coveney]

Rory and Natasha addressing a fundraising event in Cairns [photo: Andrew Coveney]

Tony gutting our rare catch [photo: Rory Coveney]

Golden Apple *being taken out of the water for a thorough cleaning* [photo: Rory Coveney]

Tony buying vital provisions in Kumai, Borneo [photo: Rory Coveney]

Rebecca with Elvis and Madé [photo: Rory Coveney]

Rebecca, Rory and Tony wrapped up [photo: Andrew Coveney]

Andrew practising with the sextant [photo: Rory Coveney]

Rebecca going into a temple in Bali. Rory and Tony dressed for the occasion! [photo: Andrew Coveney]

Tea-pickers in Sri Lanka [photo: Rory Coveney]

Tony, Rebecca, Rory and Andrew with elephants in Sri Lanka

Rebecca stitching Tony's arm en route [photo: Andrew Coveney]

Rough weather in the Red Sea [photo: Andrew Coveney]

Rory with a camel in Egypt [photo: Pauline Coveney]

Home at last. Adi Roche and Simon approaching Golden Apple
with Rebecca, Tony, Rory and Andrew on deck [photo: The Examiner]

to enjoy. Fortunately none of them found us, comparatively skinny Irish, in any way attractive so we luckily escaped unscathed.

Sunday is strictly a day of rest in the kingdom of Tonga by law. It is so strict in fact that people aren't allowed even to run generators because the noise may disturb the karma. One sailor a few years previously had been put in jail for the day for playing his stereo too loud. It was with great interest that we attended mass in the local church as Sunday mass is a huge event in the locality for everyone. People, at their slow pace, walk from miles around to attend the service. The church was absolutely bursting at the seams with all age groups. Everyone was dressed up in his or her Sunday best. The women wore incredibly colourful dresses, bright pinks and reds and oranges were everywhere. The men and boys over the age of twelve wore a woven tapa around their waists. The tapa is a traditional skirt woven from palm leaves. Mass truly was a celebration for them. The singing lifted the roof off the building rather like you would hear in the gospel churches of the southern states of America. It was as different from Irish Catholicism as it could be, although like rural Ireland it was as much a social gathering as a religious event. It appeared to us, looking in, that it was a very close-knit community.

We left Tonga and set sail for Fiji on Monday afternoon having stocked up with some fresh supplies and once again going through the ritual of officialdom with customs and immigration. It was a journey of about 650 miles in all and it was a more difficult passage than most because Tonga is in a very active volcanic area so there were many islands, shoals and reefs along the way. Andrew's navigation was severely tested. On approaching the outlying islands of Fiji we were caught with too much sail up. For those who don't know a whole lot about sailing, the amount of sail up is proportional to the amount of

wind blowing so we had to constantly adjust as conditions changed. Normally it was easy to predict with forecasts on the radio and by studying the cloud formations. But sometimes the conditions can change very quickly and unexpectedly. If too many sails are up when the wind gets strong you tend to risk breaking equipment and losing control of the boat. Of course the more sail up the faster we went so it is a constant trade-off between speed and safety. Anyway we were passing very close between two reefs when suddenly a gust came out of nowhere. We had all our sails up including the spinnaker. The boat started rolling violently and surging forward at great speed. We had to get the spinnaker down quickly and we had to do it without ripping the sail and also avoiding the reefs on either side of us. Getting the spinnaker down when the wind was really blowing required good teamwork and timing. We managed it, with difficulty, and we breathed a sigh of relief and patted ourselves on the back for not doing any damage.

Just after this the telephone rang, it was 96FM the Cork radio station, I can't really remember what I said in the interview but I was a little bit out of breath. I remember thinking afterwards what a strange way of life this must have sounded to people listening back in Cork, stuck in a traffic jam. We had a different set of worries and concerns than most other people of our age, or any age for that matter. We had been travelling for so long that it had become a way of life for us. We couldn't really remember what it was actually like to be living in a house or flat or driving a car. At times I think we all missed those simple and normal things. When we arrived home I can remember a journalist asking Tony what he missed most, and he said he would love a normal slice of toast. That might sound sort of stupid but it is just an example of what we all missed.

We arrived in Lautoka in Fiji at dawn on 14 June. Once again I was confronted with the bureaucratic mountain of

documents before we could enter the country – it took the entire day. Peter came with me to do the same for their boat and both of us laughed at the ridiculous duplication of it all, as we must have filled out the same information about six times on six different forms. Mum and Dave were due to arrive a week later and we were to head off to the remote Yasawa islands north-west of the mainland. We spent the week getting the boat looking its best for our guests. We always got very excited when we knew someone was coming to join us for a while. I also knew this was going to be a difficult time for Mum as it was the first time she was going to be on the boat without Dad. I think in some ways she wasn't really looking forward to it and the very least we all wanted was to have the boat looking as good as we could. We had become very proud of *Golden Apple,* it was as if she had, since Dad's death, become ours and we enjoyed when other people stopped to admire her and got great satisfaction out of seeing her looking her best. We began varnishing almost any wooden piece we could find on the boat as the sun had been beating down on it for months and it had begun to peel and dry up in places. We repainted all the white surfaces on the deck and cleaned the interior completely. By the time Mum and Dave arrived she looked like a new boat.

During the week we made some good friends, mainly due to being invited to their endless kava-drinking ceremonies. Like Tonga, kava is a big feature of the Fijian way of life. Everyone sits in a circle with their knees touching while the chief starts the singing and others start strumming on their guitars. Most songs were in Fijian but they insisted we sang some Irish songs. Unfortunately us Coveneys are not blessed with the ability to sing a note. We struggled through a few verses of *Molly Malone* and *Danny Boy*, Tony even dug out a Christy Moore song and they just kept in tune on their little guitars and thought we were great. Maybe they were just being polite or perhaps a little

intoxicated after their fifteenth cup of kava.

It was also the first time since back in Tahiti that we had been tied up at a dock so we were able to set up our Sail Chernobyl stall behind the boat. The harbour we were in was a big centre for tourist cruises to the islands and many people stopped and took leaflets and spoke to us about what we were doing. Many of them had never heard of Chernobyl or what was going on in Belarus and were surprised to hear the extent of the damage the accident had caused. Many of the Fijians explained how upset they had been at the nuclear testing done by the French and how powerless they felt to do anything about it. One young man told us how cousins of his who lived in the Cook Islands had rowed over a thousand miles in an open top boat to protest at the testing in Murarao Atoll. We also learned that many of the children from this small group of islands are suffering from similar diseases to those from Belarus, albeit on a smaller scale.

The four of us waited anxiously at Nadi airport for Mum and Dave to arrive. It was great when they finally came through the arrival lounge. They looked exhausted and really relieved to have arrived. Dave laughed as he explained that after twenty-four hours flying his feet were like concrete blocks, his ears were popping like mad and he was slightly tired to say the least. Mum cried a little when we got to the boat, it must have been very tough for her. After about half an hour or so she was smiling again and very happy to be with us.

The two weeks we spent in the Yasawa islands were fantastic. It's hard to believe that such places still exist on this earth, so unspoiled and untouched by development with a charm and innocence that can only come from isolation. Our time visiting the tiny settlements on the islands was really special. The gentleness and friendliness of the people here is quite humbling, they have so little to give yet they welcomed

us into their homes with open arms, as interested in us as we in them. Some of them spoke English and were fascinated about where we had travelled from and what we were doing. Everywhere we went, little kids greeted us with 'Bula', the Fijian for 'hello'. They were fascinated by our appearance and smiled at us throughout the entire church service we attended on Sunday morning in the village of Somosomo. Afterwards, outside the small village church, the children surrounded us, practising the few English words they had – 'It's very nice to meet you'.

Bill, one of the locals we shared tea with in the village of Somosomo, showed us his new-born girl of whom he was incredibly proud. He told us that he never met his own father and this saddened him a great deal. His house was more like a shed made of corrugated iron and wood, it had no furniture, we all sat on the ground feeling somewhat uncomfortable that we might be intruding. He talked for a long time about his life and his children and wife. Before we left we took some photos of him with Juliana (his wife) and their new child and we gave him the film to get developed on the mainland. These people loved photos; there were pictures of Princess Diana in almost every home we went to.

On each island we greeted the chief with a gift of a kava root which is the traditional way of asking permission to spend some time on their island. It was accepted on each occasion with great ceremony involving some type of Fijian prayer and clapping of the hands. It was a very serious ritual but I have to admit we did find it a little amusing although we did our best to remain solemn.

The food on these islands was almost all from the sea. One night we decided to have dinner in one of the small backpacker hostels. We were presented with various sea creatures that had been caught that day including octopus, clams, crabs and some other unrecognisable fish. Even the vegetables were

a form of seaweed that tasted like salty cabbage. Normally we are not very adventurous eaters but we were determined to try everything. The long octopus tentacles with their rubbery suckers were not a pretty sight. I managed to scrape them and found nice white meat on the inside that tasted, to my surprise, very good. Dave was not so fortunate and could not eat a thing. He just watched us in amazement and dreamed of his bread and Nutella on the boat. Mum was the only one who dared to try the local giant clams or should I say clam as she only had one and found herself swigging her bottle of beer to try to lose the taste and she felt exceedingly ill after it. These clam things looked repulsive, like big purple lips. Apparently every island in this area has a sacred fish and octopus was the speciality here. We met the rather withered-looking old lady who catches the octopuses – in fact that is her only job.

We left Fiji on 30 June and headed for Vanuatu. The crossing was one that combined absolute flat calms and heavy winds. As we sailed for the first few days Mum said to me that anybody could do this as she was lying in the sun under the gentle winds. She was to eat her words a day later when we were all over the place and waves were crashing over the deck. She wouldn't come out of her cabin and we just kept passing cups of tea down to her. Tony spent the voyage trying to improve his fishing techniques. He had been battling to catch a fish since Mum and Dave arrived but had been unsuccessful for nearly three weeks, it was driving him mad because he wanted to cook a fish for Mum. Just before we entered Port Vila harbour in Vanuatu on the evening of Saturday 4 July he finally managed, to sounds of great rejoicing, to pull in a tuna. After we had anchored in the harbour he cooked up a great meal.

Sunday was a little frustrating for everyone. While I went ashore to negotiate with immigration, customs and the general

health authorities the rest were forced to sit it out on the boat tantalisingly close to a nice long walk on land or maybe even an ice cream. Officially when arriving in port, nobody is allowed to step on land until we had been cleared in. Being a Sunday, the whole process was extremely slow, so it wasn't until late afternoon that everyone was allowed to go ashore. Port Vila, the capital of this very young country, self-ruling since 1980, was surprisingly busy. It was quite commercialised with several banks and businesses. We were told that the rest of the islands that make up this country were very different and much more under-developed than even the remotest parts of Fiji or Tonga.

The immense variety of Vanuatu's culture and customs is reflected in the existence of 105 indigenous languages among a population of only 150,000. Most islands have their own distinct customs and artistic styles. Sorcery and magic are practised widely in the non-Christian parts of Vanuatu. In some communities a woman is sometimes honoured, in a public ceremony which may last a few hours, by having a front tooth smashed out with a rock by the village tooth remover, after she has slaughtered several pigs with her bare hands. Many of the young women we saw in the market didn't have any front teeth. Cannibalism was regular among rival tribes during the last century and while both France and Britain ruled. The last known case of cannibalism is as late as 1969 and these tribes still live high in the hills today. Vanuatu is also the place where the first bungee jumps were ever carried out. In one of the northern most islands it is still custom for young boys and men to prove their bravery by jumping off progressively higher platforms with vines tied to their ankles.

A giant cockroach landed on the boat on our second night in Port Vila. We were eating dinner in the cockpit when Andy heard this bang behind his head and he thought someone had

thrown a stone onto the deck. When he turned around he saw this giant flying roach, about ten centimetres long. Both Mum and Bec started screaming madly when they saw it. Andy in a typically calm manner managed to put a glass over it to stop it going down below. I managed to get a photograph of the giant beast before we threw it over the side. We were all relieved to have it over the side as we had been having cockroach problems on the boat for a long while but had seen nothing this size.

Unfortunately we didn't get a chance to explore any of the other islands. We did however get a chance to do a spectacular dive over a deep-water wreck the day before we headed for Australia. We had all learned how to dive. Rebecca and I had been trained in Ireland before we left and the lads had taken a course while we were in the Caribbean.

The shipwreck was 40 metres down so it was a little daunting at first as none of us had ever been that deep before. The wreck was a 200-ft cargo ship called *Semina* and she looked amazing as she emerged out of the big blue the further down we went. It was the second time I had been over a wreck and I found it a little scary – they look so out of place and sad lying under the water. All sorts of fish were swimming in and out of her portholes and around the big propeller at the stern. We saw a few barracudas, shoals of brightly coloured fish and even a sea snake. No sharks, thank God. I had yet to see a shark under the water, I'm not sure how I would react if I did. We couldn't stay down at that depth for long as the deeper it is the more air you use. After about ten minutes we started our ascent. It was lucky that we did as I was very low on air and had to share the instructor's air half way back to the surface. I think the cigarettes must have made a difference, as everyone else seemed to be fine. I was very relieved to get to the surface.

Mum and Dave left that afternoon by plane and we were to see them again in Australia in a few weeks time. That night

we went out for dinner with Peter and Melanie, they were heading to Sydney and we were going to Cairns so it was unlikely that we would see them again. Like when we were saying goodbye to Eric we were upset, as they had become good friends.

The South Pacific had been one of the most amazing places I think I will ever be lucky enough to visit. In the space of two months we had been to five small countries that are literally miles from the rest of the world out in the middle of the largest ocean on the planet. In this group of tiny islands lie some of my best memories of the voyage and as we headed for the new continent of Australia we were delighted we had decided to resume this epic journey. As a crew we had developed well and despite some early frictions between us, we all worked well together and we had adapted well to being one crew member down.

8

HALF-WAY

Australia was to prove my happiest and busiest part of the whole trip. It was when we had reached the half-way stage of the journey. We had crossed two of the world's greatest oceans and we all felt a great sense of achievement. After Australia we were on our way home and every mile after that was going to be towards achieving our ultimate goal. We were also meeting up with our brother Patrick and his new fiancée Emma who were taking a sort of pre-wedding honeymoon to come and see us. We hadn't seen Patrick since the funeral and were looking forward to seeing him in happier times. Mum and Dave were also going to be there for a couple of days before heading home.

But for more than any other reason I was happy because it was here that I met up with my girlfriend again. I had met Thea in college the year before I left, and had been falling for her in a big way. She always made me laugh and she had, like me, the ability to talk about ideas and theories for hours and hours. Our relationship was something that I missed very much during the five months at sea and particularly during those horrible days at home back in March. The trip had stopped a really cool time between us and instead of being resentful she was very encouraging from the beginning. She had been there at the very early stages of the planning and had never let her feelings for me get in the way of what she knew could mean the end of a great time for both of us. For this I loved her more than anything else. We had tentatively agreed to meet up when I got to Australia. She was working in Sydney for about six months before we were due to arrive, and to be honest I didn't know

what to expect when I saw her in Cairns. We had talked on the phone every now and then but seven months is a long time to be apart and so much can change that I was very nervous before we met. It's unlike me to be nervous like that but I was hoping that things would be the same when we met again.

We hadn't had much luck with the fishing since leaving Vanuatu, at least until we tried some new tactics. Three days before we reached Cairns I was up early and happened to look over the side of the boat and through sleepy eyes I saw a shoal of about 30 Rainbow Runners sheltering under the boat so I decided to do my utmost to catch one. Surely, I thought, with them so close I'd manage to hook just one. At first I tried to tempt them by dragging our most cherished lure on the surface of the water right above them. One of them made a dart for it, grabbed it, but got away again. I was becoming frustrated when no others seemed in any way interested in the lure. I loaded up the spear-gun and leaned over the back of the boat with it. The magnificent yellow-tailed fish swam only a few inches below the water. Their turquoise backs glistened in the early morning sun. Tony and Andy had joined me at this stage to watch and could barely withstand the suspense. The spear had a rope tied to it so if I managed to get the spear into one I would need to hold on.

'Go on Ror, Go on,' Andy whispered. 'Don't take one too big or you'll never hold on!'

I gradually built up enough courage and eventually I shot. It went straight through the middle of a three-foot long fish and then the struggle pursued. I held on to the gun for dear life. The unfortunate fish put up a terrible struggle but I managed, with some wrestling, to haul him onto the deck. Tony had him gutted and filleted within about ten minutes. Naturally I could not resist gloating over my new 'Hot Shot Hamish' status.

When we arrived into Cairns harbour we were met by

Patrick holding up some Big Macs from McDonalds. We had phoned before we arrived and asked him if he could get us a few burgers as we had run out of most of our food and were starving. It was great to see Pat and the others. He was as usual wearing one of his horrible gaudy bright shirts – some things never change. He seemed to be back to his usual self since the last time we had seen him. The four of us munched our burgers. It took some time to clear in with the authorities and I think they were a little put out that I was eating a Big Mac as I filled in the various forms. Australia has some of the strictest quarantine regulations in the world. The various officers that boarded the boat confiscated all that remained of our vegetables and took any canned meats. They even took our drinking chocolate because it contained dried milk. The whole thing was a bit ridiculous, but it didn't bother me a whole lot – I had grown quite used to over-zealous officials.

The following day I was waiting in the airport for nearly two hours. I had got the time of Thea's flight wrong and was much too early. Rebecca had been joking with me about how nervous I was before I went to the airport, I shrugged it off, but she really had no idea that I was genuinely very excited and a little worried. Eventually the monitor showed that the plane from Sydney had arrived, and I paced around trying to appear calm and distant and not too anxious. After yet another trip to the toilet I made a quick dash for another cigarette in an effort to calm myself further. Then I saw her strolling down the corridor just as I remembered her with a big smile and looking slightly fussed. It was nice that I could see she was nervous, at least it wasn't just me. We hugged and the two of us not really knowing what to say just laughed nervously and kissed again and again – not really knowing what to expect from each other and it was easier than trying to say anything. I couldn't really believe her shoes, they were massive platform type things, they

looked kind of funny and I couldn't resist commenting on them, it wasn't so much the shoes as the tiny white socks that peeped above them. She thumped me when I made a joke about them, but she didn't seem annoyed or embarrassed. We left the airport and rather than join the others back at the boat we went into town for a beer that both of us needed.

We all went out for dinner that night. It was the last night we were going to see Mum and Dave until Christmas so we were all a little upset. I think they had really enjoyed their time with us and I knew Mum had been very apprehensive about coming out to the boat. She had never sailed on a long passage before but she had done fantastically well on our trip from Fiji to Vanuatu and even when she was scared she was always in good spirits. Once again for me she had shown her remarkable strength and courage in a year that would have broken many people. The following day was a sad one and what made it hard for us was that we were in the middle of an interview with the local television network about Sail Chernobyl the moment she came to say goodbye. I think, in a strange way, it made it easier for her to say goodbye to us quickly. I am sure at this stage she was sick of these goodbyes and it was good that we were distracted.

Patrick and Emma were to be with us for about a week before heading back to London. Pat was keen to do a bit of sailing as it had been over a year since he had been on the boat. The plan was to head to the Whitsunday Islands about a hundred miles south of Cairns for a couple of days and then to work our way back up again. It was funny to see Patrick and Emma so completely in love. It was strange to think that Pat would be leaving the family soon to start his own – everything was changing so fast. For us, on the boat, it was hard to imagine all the changes that were going on at home. I think we all hoped that things would be the same when we got back while

at the same time knew they wouldn't be.

Patrick told us that Simon was thinking of standing in the by-election for Dad's seat in Dáil Éireann. I wasn't sure about what to think as over the years we had all seen both the good and bad sides of politics and knew intimately the pressures and restrictions of life under the public eye. I was worried for Simon – did he fully understand that his life would be so radically altered? When I spoke to him on the phone I knew that he really wanted to go for it and he seemed remarkably determined and very sure that this was what he wanted to do. The election was set for November.

The trip down to the Whitsunday's turned out to be a nightmare as the weather was awful and the wind was blowing from the wrong direction. After two days trying we gave up and decided to stay around the Cairns area. I think Emma was relieved that we abandoned our efforts to go south, as she tends to get seasick. Luckily we did get some nice weather then and both Patrick and Emma had an enjoyable few days before heading back to London to work. It was great to speak to Patrick at length about how things were at home. Since Dad died he had become the head of the family and it was very reassuring to know that he had everything under control. I too had worries, like lots of people, about what I was going to do when I got home and he came up with some good options and helped me with my CV. It was hard to imagine what it would be like to be working normal hours in an office given what we were doing. I wondered what a prospective employer would make of a CV like mine.

Thea seemed to enjoy the sailing and I was relieved that she didn't get seasick. She had only been on the boat once before, a weekend trip to Kinsale, and it didn't involve any real sailing. Some people find it very difficult to sleep while at sea but she slept like a baby in her bunk. She has a really odd way

of sleeping, she lies on her back with her feet crossed and her hands crossed on her stomach. Inside the small bunk she looked very peaceful and content with a little smile, almost dead, like an Egyptian Mummy as the boat rolled around in the waves.

We had to do some long overdue repairs to the boat. We had left many things unfixed as we knew we would have time here to repair them so we took *Golden Apple* out of the water to repaint the bottom and to change the angle of the propeller to give us more speed under engine. The process of taking the boat out of the water was a nerve-wracking event. *Golden Apple* weighs nearly thirty tons and the travel-lift crane was only capable of lifting forty tons and this was the heaviest boat that the boat yard in Cairns had ever lifted. There was a terrifying sound of creaking as the boat came out of the water. She looked terribly vulnerable as she crossed over the concrete. We were all relieved to see her safely perched up on the stakes. Luckily the man was fairly relaxed about the manoeuvre which helped to calm us all. He looked like one of the Sex Pistols with a blond Mohican haircut and numerous tattoos, but seemed to know his job well. We were out of the water for three days and were very busy with painting and repairs. I even managed to get Thea to do some sanding which was a little difficult considering she doesn't relish physical labour, she just kept laughing at me covered in paint and dust and all in all wasn't very effective with the sandpaper.

We were also keen if possible to hold some sort of fundraiser while in Australia. Almost as soon as we got back to Cairns from our trip down the coast with Patrick we met Ivan and Natasha, a Ukrainian couple. They were musicians and came up with the idea of maybe organising a fundraising concert. They had seen the Sail Chernobyl flag flying on the boat and had wondered what it was all about. Natasha had been in Kiev in 1986 and knew many people who had been directly

affected by the Chernobyl disaster. She told me she had picked up her young cousins from the train station in Kiev. The train had come from Minsk and as the train stopped in the station about fifty men, dressed in protective suits, hosed it down while all the passengers remained inside not really knowing what was going on. They were ordered to leave their shoes on the platform before they left the station so as not to bring any contaminated soil or dust with them. Natasha told me her little cousins had no idea what had happened in Chernobyl – the three of them fell seriously sick in the months following the accident. After the twins had explained to them what the whole project was about they agreed to help.

Cairns was the first place we were going to stay for a decent amount of time so we decided it would be good if we broke up for a while. I think we all needed a break from the boat and each other. After we put the boat back in the water the twins decided they were going to head off to Sydney and then onto Ayers Rock for about a week and a half. Thea, Rebecca and I stayed on in Cairns to try, with the help of Ivan and Natasha, to get the concert organised.

Ivan was a hippie and a dreamer, the concert was his idea and I don't think it would ever have happened without his enthusiasm. However he was a nightmare to work with. He was one of those people who have about fifty ideas a day – one that might be useful – but no real understanding of how any of them could be achieved. We had only two weeks to organise everything. In the end we broke up the tasks quite clearly. He would organise the bands and the music system and we, the crew, would do everything else from publicity to the invitations, to organising the venue and bar. Natasha was the opposite of Ivan and very able but she was almost seven months pregnant so couldn't really do a whole lot.

The concert date was set for Friday, 21 August, two days

before we were due to head off again for Darwin. Thea and I decided to rent a car and head off for the weekend before that and spent a fantastic couple of days up in Port Douglas and Cape Tribulation, north of Cairns. We spent time on the beach and swam in the sea, checked out the koalas and both agreed that they were very funny animals. We went on a crocodile-spotting boat trip and felt like we were real nerds, given the average age on the boat was about seventy. The other people looked like something out of a Gary Larson comic strip, big-hipped and narrow shouldered. We only saw one crocodile who merely yawned in the sun. We stayed in spectacular Eco-style forest guesthouses that overlooked the Daintree rain forest and river. Port Douglas was a beautiful little town; it was much smaller than Cairns and prettier. But I think the nicest thing about it was the little white church in the park that overlooked the sea. In comparison to many churches this was remarkably simple. Behind the altar there was a huge window that opened out onto the blue water and it looked stunning in the morning sun. It was great to just be on our own for a while and not to have to worry about the boat. We talked and joked for hours and got drunk on red wine. We laughed real laughs and shared dreams and hopes. It was a special time.

When we got back to Cairns Tony and Andy had returned from their travels and we all started to get the concert organised once again. The venue for the event had been finalised and we had paid over the fee. It was a massive old diesel tank that was used during the Second World War for refuelling warships. The tanks had been refurbished with lights, a stage, etc., and the interior looked sort of spooky but it had a great atmosphere. The idea was for the event to be both educational and entertaining. It was to be a multimedia event with simultaneous video and slide photograph images with live music. The aim was to try to capture people emotionally with the problems in

Belarus. It was a difficult enough aim as Australians, and particularly Queenslanders, are not the most emotional of people.

On the Wednesday before the concert Andy and I spoke at the university for an hour about the problems in Belarus. I was nervous about it but it went well and the thirty or forty people who came seemed to be genuinely interested. They were shocked at many of the photographs and couldn't believe the damage that a disaster that had happened twelve years previously could have caused, and was still causing. Most of them agreed to come to the concert and lend their support.

A good friend of mine joined the boat in that week before the concert. When I had been at home after Dad's funeral I had asked him if he was free would he like to come out to the boat for a while. Owen was going to be with us as far as Singapore. I had gone across Australia a few years previously with him and another friend of ours. That trip had taken about two months in a car, so I knew he would be well able for the journey and the stresses that living in a small space would place on him. There are very few people any of us could think of who could do a trip like this. It's not that people wouldn't enjoy parts of it, it's just that the length of time it takes to go the whole way around the world means that it becomes a way of life rather than a holiday.

The concert wasn't as much of a success as we had hoped. The venue looked fantastic but we didn't get a big turnout. We raised about £1,000 but had hoped for a lot more. All those who came really enjoyed themselves as the show went well and I think people were very moved by the images and music.

Overall our stay in Cairns had been a good one. While we hadn't raised huge funds we had raised considerable awareness for our project. Between us, we had been on two television networks – one of them national – and every local radio station, as well as three national radio stations. I think many

people who had never heard of Chernobyl at least now knew about many of the problems. We had also managed to fix everything on the boat, even our freezer that had been broken for months: Tony was delighted, at least now we could store a good quantity of meat.

Thea left on the Sunday night for Ireland via New Zealand and we were both upset to be leaving each other again. We had had a great time and neither of us wanted it to end. It is difficult now, at home, to write about that time with her because things didn't work out between us – but for a time we were blissfully happy together, and as she would put it, she completely rocked my world.

We departed for Darwin on Monday evening. It was good to be back at sea again after our long stay in Cairns, each mile now was a mile closer to Ireland rather than further away. Between Cairns and Darwin lie some of the most treacherous sailing waters in the world. We sailed inside the Great Barrier Reef as far as the northern most point of Australia which certainly put Andrew, our navigator, through his paces. We were a bit apprehensive to say the least. There were reefs everywhere, some of which are uncharted and this made the need for a keen eye even greater than before. There were ships everywhere, which added to the difficulty of the passage, and in such a narrow channel we had to keep an ear to the radio and our eyes peeled. It was strange to be sailing in waters little more than eight metres deep and with land and reefs on either side of us. Coming across the Pacific we were rarely in waters shallower than about two thousand metres.

Our new crew member Owen was settling in well. We were a bit embarrassed as he was revolutionising fishing on board – on the second day he had caught three fish. It made a big difference having an extra person on the boat, particularly at night as now we could all get a few extra hours of sleep.

Andy didn't cook very much on the boat but when he did he only ever cooked his one and only dish – chicken curry. While Andy has many talents cooking is certainly not one of them, every time he cooks this dish he insists on putting loads of mayonnaise into it no matter how much we tell him that it does nothing for the taste. Another night he decided to cook lasagna but much to our amusement instead of putting pasta on the top layer he decided to sprinkle it with uncooked rice. He really never failed to make everyone feel a little on edge health-wise when he dared to cook something.

Speaking of rice we were having a real nightmare with our stores. We had bought giant sacks of rice in the Pacific but now had a real battle on our hands with the bugs that had invaded our stocks. The little beggars were just about the same size as a grain of rice so we couldn't just sieve them out. They were black and the only way to catch them was as they floated to the surface during cooking. I think they are called weevils. Tony only decided to tell us this when most of the supplies had gone and after we had been eating this weevil-infested rice for months.

Rebecca celebrated her twentieth birthday on the trip to Darwin. Tony cooked up a special chocolate cake for the occasion and we even had a few candles to put on top. We left her off her night-watch duty that night as well as giving her a few small presents we'd bought in Cairns. Rebecca had changed very much during the previous year. I remember at the beginning people thought that the two of us would fight the most but we got on really well. I would always joke with her that she was 'learning all the time' and she was, as we all were. Perhaps for her the changes were more pronounced. She had never been away from home before and must have been at times very lonely away from all her friends. She had become very independent. I suppose living with four brothers would be a real test for any girl. For me Rebecca had always been my baby

sister but she was now becoming a real friend, and oddly we were perhaps becoming closer than I was with either of the twins. For her birthday I bought her *Lord of the Rings* which I thought might help fill those long night-watches with the wondrous tales of Frodo and his little friends.

The day before we arrived in Darwin it was flat calm and incredibly hot. We decided to stop the boat and jump in for a swim to cool off. Rebecca refused because she's terrified of sharks. It turned out to be a very wise decision indeed. We were only out of the water about twenty seconds when a six-foot Hammerhead shark swam out from under the boat. We had been told that sharks sometimes tend to swim underneath boats out of the sun – apparently they can stay there for hours. We couldn't believe how lucky we had been.

Rebecca's boyfriend Owen and Andrew's girlfriend Mimi joined us in Darwin. They were going to be with us as far as Bali. Both Bec and Andy were delighted, of course now it was my turn to tease Rebecca about her nervousness. She took about two hours to get ready before going to the airport. Andy was a little nervous as well but unlike the rest of us he has an ability to conceal these things pretty well.

Darwin was for me the place I wouldn't really return to in a hurry. We were there for a week and I had come to the conclusion that I didn't really like rural Australians. Of course there were some that I liked but unfortunately those dreadful stereotypes of the vest-wearing, loud, racist, and chauvinist Australian male were plentiful in Darwin.

To our surprise we bumped into *Madjk* again while moored at the marina in Darwin. Once we had left them way back in the San Blas Islands we never thought we would see them again. Mike told me that they had decided to skip going to New Zealand and had made up the time. They were all in good spirits and full of news of the Pacific. They too had had a wonderful

time there. Amy's parents were over to visit for a few weeks and they were all leaving their boat and heading down to Sydney. Keegan proudly told me that he was ahead with his schoolwork. We agreed to meet up with them again in Bali before heading in to the dangerous waters of the South China Sea which, like the coast of Colombia, is notorious for pirate attacks. We thought it would be good to travel together as far as Singapore and we were all looking forward to a whole new frontier in Asia.

9

A New Frontier

The fundraising hadn't been going that well. We had reached many people with the story of Chernobyl but we were still a long way short of our financial target. With the exception of Australia most of the countries we had been in were very poor and weren't places where we could raise money. Asia was going to be just as poor so we had to rethink how we were going to improve our efforts. While awareness is important, money is what would make the real difference in Belarus. We hadn't received the corporate support we had hoped for so we were going to have to find an alternative way to use what we were doing to raise money.

Our internet site had grown considerably in popularity since we had left. Our sponsors Aardvark in Cork were doing a fantastic job of constantly changing and updating it. We were getting hundreds of messages of support on the site from people all over the world, mostly from children. It was becoming clear that children, in particular younger children, were finding the site and the voyage very interesting and exciting. So we, in conjunction with our project co-ordinator and PR team at home, decided to focus our efforts into turning the website into an educational tool geared to capturing the imagination of schoolchildren and their teachers. If we could attract the schools to the project we hoped that they might, in turn, raise money. It helped a great deal that Mimi, our project co-ordinator, was herself a teacher and understood what teachers liked and could use in the classroom. The move towards computers beginning in schools also helped. After much negotiation, between Mimi and Simon with the Minister for Education

and Scoilnet the department's website people, it was agreed that the Sail Chernobyl website would be used as the introductory website for schools all over Ireland. Mimi put together a pack that included a map and literature and it was sent to over 4,500 schools around the country. Our daily updates were now being read by far more people and interest was growing. Many schools began doing all sorts of things to raise money – from penalty shoot-outs, to fancy dress to sponsored walks and the total was beginning to rise. On the boat we began to receive emails from children asking questions about how we were getting on.

◊

We were all really excited wondering what Asia would be like. Our first stop was on the tiny island of Roti, just south of Timor, in Indonesia. The trip from Darwin had been frustrating. We had no wind and had to motor the whole way so we were very low on fuel. We had originally planned to go straight to Bali but I was worried we wouldn't have enough fuel, so we stopped to try to refuel.

The island was surrounded by reef and there was a huge swell breaking as we passed into the small lagoon where a few other boats were anchored. There were lots of people out surfing; Indonesia is a favourite place for many of the Australian surfers searching for the ultimate wave. I remembered when I had tried to surf during my time working in Australia I had been hopeless and spent much of the time either half drowning or swimming after my board. I had managed to get up once or twice and it was a great feeling to be hurtling down the face of a breaking wave, completely out of control, and screaming like an idiot but I decided it wasn't something that was worth near death half of the time. Owen was delighted with the prospect of having another go at it, he had been in Australia with me

and was a competent surfer. After we anchored the boat he headed for the waves and the rest of us went into the village in search of fuel and some fresh supplies.

The most striking difference in the people was their size. The whole way across the Pacific and Australia people had been big but here, much like the Indians back in Panama, the people were very small. The houses were nearly all made from wood and corrugated iron and were clustered together under the massive coconut trees, a little like the villages in the Yasawa Islands in Fiji. There were some cars but mainly scooters and small motor-bikes. The roads didn't have any tarmac and were only sandy paths through the trees. It was almost impossible to communicate. While it had been difficult in other places here we didn't even know how to say hello. The signs were completely incomprehensible to us and it was a little like being dropped on a different planet. We did manage to get our fuel and some bread and fruit with some difficulty and by drawing pictures. They were a friendly people even if timid at first and were glad to get our dollars.

We left for Bali after our short two-day stay in Roti. It was incredibly hot on the boat and we all were finding it difficult to sleep at night. I wrote the following in a letter to a friend of mine as we made our way towards Bali: 'Yesterday the fan that blows onto my bed broke, I know it may sound extravagant to you to have a fan blowing onto the bed, but believe me when I say I need it. It's so hot and humid here that any movement above a walk and you start sweating uncontrollably. I don't think our Irish skins were designed for these conditions. Imagine getting into bed in a sauna, lying down covered in sweat and slipping around in the bed because you can't stop sweating and the whole thing is moving, then imagine a little fan blowing cold air onto your face, how good it would feel, good enough perhaps to even sleep, then imagine someone turning off the air – that was me

last night sliding around my bed in a quite disgusting lather of perspiration! I slept for about one hour and was quite relieved when my watch came so I could go up on deck. I have spent the day trying to fix my little fan, but I think it is burnt out, all is not lost however as I have managed to steal a replacement from the bunk next to the engine room that is free since Simon isn't here. So tonight hopefully I will be able to catch some sleep.'

We arrived in Bali on my birthday, 19 September. I had been to Bali before and it was amazing how the smell of a place can seem so familiar after so many years. It was the smell of the tobacco that they smoke. There are people everywhere. It is a huge tourist centre and the whole place is geared towards this massive tourist trade. Shopping for anything here is a real experience. Although everything is very cheap whatever you buy will cost you a great deal of sweat and an inevitable loss of patience. Every price is open to discussion and barter and initially this can be somewhat amusing but after a while it can become somewhat draining. If you're into watches this is the place to come. Walk down any street here and you'll be greeted with a minimum of a dozen vendors trying to persuade you to buy a watch you really don't want. At first I generally just said 'no thank you' but I quickly learned that the best policy was to simply ignore the oncoming salesmen and walk on.

Tony was finding it difficult to sleep at night. He decided to sleep out in the open air up on deck. While the dreaded mosquitoes were annoying he decided the wind and the open air would be much cooler than down in the cabin. He slept well until 2.30am when he was woken by a flash of lightning and a great downpour of rain. He tried to ignore it at first, in that classic way one tends to hope vainly things will go away, but once he could feel the water running into his sleeping bag that was enough. He dashed for the cover of the cabin. We all woke

up as we saw him bundling down the hatch with his soaking sleeping-bag and dripping pillow. The rest of us found it amusing as he had thought he had solved the heat issue and after much cajoling he too began to laugh at the situation.

We stayed in Bali for a week or so, the boat as usual needed lots of work. The hot sun was really eating into the varnish so we decided again to catch up on some much-needed varnish work. We did take time to do a tour of the island, which brought us out of the tourist areas. The countryside was very lush and there were many rice fields terraced on the hills like steps. Religious worship is a part of life in Bali and the Hindu temple we visited had a constant stream of thousands of locals. Many brought gifts to the temple – little baskets with flowers and fruit and vegetables. The women were dressed in highly ornate robes in bright pinks and oranges. We had to wear a robe around our waists as we climbed the steps to see the highly ornate temple. Religion seemed, to me at least, very important to the people, and many had walked miles to this central temple in the hills. It was amazing to see a smaller version of the temples in each of the homes we passed as we travelled around the island. This devotion fascinated me and seemed to make our so-called land of saints in Ireland almost heathen. Religion in this part of the world appeared to be a great unifying force.

Indonesia was in the middle of an election when we were there. Although Indonesian politics is not something I know a great deal about it was interesting to see the process that I am so familiar with at home. Election campaigns had always been a feature of our life as we grew up, we were as immersed in politics as we were in the sea. The party canvassing in Ireland attempts to be persuasive on an individual level at each doorstep. It is a very personal process with a relatively small population where there is a good chance that you might actually know the candidate or at least have met him or her. Here it was

quite the opposite. It was all about mass appeal and branding in the most basic sense, almost like a football team. There were red flags everywhere, massive flags, the candidate's symbol was the bull's head. At one point we were passed by the candidate's motorcade that took the form of hundreds of mopeds trailing these huge flags from their aerials. I thought it wasn't so much canvassing as hysteria and propaganda. This was the only way to run a campaign here as the population was so large and the electorate disparate. There are over 200 million people, with hundreds of languages and at least five different forms of religious worship, living in over 13,000 islands stringing over thousands of miles of ocean. A political nightmare, in many ways ungovernable.

Rebecca and Andy were upset to see their respective boyfriend and girlfriend head back home from Bali. Bec was a bit down: 'I miss home a lot lately listening to Owen talking about going back to college and how he can't wait to meet all his friends again. Sometimes I wish I was just doing the things most 20 year olds do but then again it feels great doing something that bit different from everyone else.'

I think we all felt this way at times particularly when people came and went. While we were all excited about our adventures, normality is very reassuring and we all missed it.

Madjk arrived two days before we were due to leave. They had had a good trip down to Sydney and were anxious to head off again. They were flying home for Christmas from Singapore and wanted to get there quickly to organise someone to look after their boat. I agreed with Mike to stay in radio contact every few hours, just to let each other know of any possible pirate activity or suspicious looking boats. Mike carried a gun on his boat, in fact most of the American boats did, to use in the event of being threatened. There are two schools of thought on the gun issue. We had decided against it, mainly because of the

difficulty we would have in each of the ports if we had one. I also thought it would be pointless if we were attacked, to start shooting, inevitably we would be out-gunned or end up shooting one of ourselves. Any pirate, worth his salt so to speak, would have lots of guns and would unlike us have no hesitation in using them.

We left Bali on 30 September for the small town of Kumai in Kalimantan, Borneo. *Madjk* wasn't going to stop here so we hoped we would meet again in Singapore. It was about halfway and we kept in radio contact for that portion of the trip at least. Kalimantan is the southern two-thirds of the island of Borneo with a population of about nine million mostly living along its rivers and mountains. We had heard from other sailors that this area, known as Tanjung Puting National Park, is incredibly interesting with a vast variety of animals including crocodiles, wild pigs, bear cats, orang-utans, monkeys, dolphins, python snakes and things called mudskippers – a kind of fish that can walk and breathe on land. The park is most famous for its orang-utans as two rehabilitation camps were set up to help this endangered species. The orang-utans in Kalimantan are the only great apes outside Africa and because the female only gives birth every eight years they are vulnerable to extinction. We were all excited about this stop-over as no one was sure what to expect. I had visions of monkeys swinging in the trees and snakes slithering around our feet with Tarzan type people living in wooden huts saying 'welcome to the jungle' in some strange language.

A day out from Kumai an extremely dodgy-looking Indonesian fishing trawler altered course and headed towards us. When it was about 200 metres away it slowed down and continued to follow us for about an hour. Fortunately there was a decent breeze so we were able to keep up eight knots with both the sails and engine, although I'd say he could have caught us

if he tried for long enough. We were all anxious, and rather ridiculously made ourselves look as imposing and tough as we could by strutting around the deck flexing our muscles. Owen was particularly menacing looking with his new skinhead haircut. Whether our macho antics made any difference or not I don't know but after an hour or so they decided to leave us alone. Unfortunately we did do some damage in the engine room in an effort to pull away from the boat. I had revved the motor a little too much and all the belts running off the front of it broke. Andy and I were going to have to spend a few hours in the engine room once again when we arrived.

In addition to the threat from piracy there was quite a lot of debris in the water in this area. Borneo is a major hardwood exporter and many of the logs seem to fall off the boats transporting them to Singapore and other centres. We had close calls on a few occasions with some of these huge logs and branches, which are submerged just below the surface and difficult to see. A large tree trunk or plank could cause us severe damage so we had to keep a sharp look-out, especially at night.

We arrived unscathed in Kumai on 3 October. It was a strange port entrance in that we had to travel some fifteen miles up the Kumai River before we reached the town. The water was a dark brown colour from the vegetation and silt being washed down from the jungle. The banks of the river were heavily wooded and it appeared like a great canopy that stretched as far as we could see. There was only one other foreign boat here and about two hundred native boats, part of a huge fishing trade. These boats were a remarkable shape, much like a banana with the bow and stern much higher than the middle. The boats had many people on them and as far as we could see from all the washing and clothes hanging these were their homes.

Within five minutes of arriving two native boats were out to greet us. We were persuaded to go on a small boat tour into

the rain forest to see the world famous orang-utans and we were due to head off for two days the following day. We all went into the town to have a look and we were a real novelty here as many people looked at us as if they had never seen a white person before. It was a very poor place and many of the houses were falling down or rotten. Most of the toilets were simply platforms out onto the river. There didn't seem to be any running water and all washing was done in the river. The shops sold really odd selections of stuff, from Bic razors to watermelons, to car tyres. Most of the packet or canned food were months out of date. Like Bali virtually everyone travelled either on foot or by motor-bike.

I had to go to the local police station to clear in with the authorities so I headed off with our guide in a rented van to the nearby town, some twenty miles away. We came across a horrendous road accident on the way. Two young boys on a moped had crashed head on into the front of an oncoming bus. As we arrived I could see a massive pool of blood on the road and to my surprise the mangled bodies were lying on the side of the road, it was very disturbing to see such lack of respect for the dead. Our driver asked one of the locals how long ago it had happened and he said the accident had occurred an hour previously. Both my guide and the driver looked visibly ill by the sight and I must say I wasn't feeling the best either. It's amazing how much we take for granted in Ireland. We are so used to basic services that it is almost impossible to imagine being without them unless you have a chance to see first-hand what everyday life is like in this type of place. Somehow human life here seemed to be less valuable.

The boat trip into the jungle was a fantastic experience. I think Bec really enjoyed it despite her misgivings about the creepy crawly situation. There is every imaginable small creature living in the jungle – snakes, spiders, cockroaches, beetles

and giant ants. Rebecca hates all these things and became almost hysterical on the boat at the sight of a cockroach. As we made our way up the river in our little boat we teased her by touching her leg at which she would jump out of her skin. This is what she wrote in her diary of the first day: 'Our tour guide gave us a briefing on the wildlife we're expected to see. I didn't ask about spiders but I'm sure the deadly ones are here as well. The boat we're travelling in is small and to me it looks a bit flimsy particularly if 5m crocs are swimming around the place. The guide assured us that they'd never attack the boat. At night apparently you can see their eyes glistening just above the water. Spooky stuff really. The orang-utans will be the highlight for me mainly because they're friendly and cuddly kind of creatures and at least you can be sure they won't eat you! All they eat is bananas.'

The boat we took was about twelve metres long but only two metres wide with just enough room below deck to kneel. We spent most of the time on the roof examining the river banks and scanning the trees on either side for monkeys. It was all very Indiana Jonesy. We travelled about twenty-five miles in total upriver from where *Golden Apple* was anchored into the depths of the jungle. We had three locals on the boat with us, the captain, the cook and 'Jean' our guide. They were all very friendly and spoke good English.

On the first day we visited a camp which was a rehabilitation centre for orphaned orang-utans. The rangers try to re-introduce them back into the wild. We couldn't believe our eyes when this huge female came bounding out of the dense undergrowth towards us with a tiny baby clinging to her back. We were more than slightly alarmed. There were two one-year-old babies playing in the bushes next to us also. The rangers had named them Elvis and Madé and while they couldn't sing they were well able to shake it in the small trees. The orang-

we finally made it back to the boat. Andy had a leech stuck to his foot, which I burned off with my cigarette lighter.

When the rain eventually stopped Andy and I paddled a dug-out canoe a mile or two upstream. The dug-out canoeing looked much easier than we thought and after almost falling out a few times we managed to make some progress. We heard all sorts of noises coming from the swampy river banks. It was a little creepy. When we returned to the camp there were two orang-utans right next to the boat. I went up to the smaller one and he grabbed on to my hand and refused to let go. They have an amazing grip from holding on to trees all day. He was remarkably friendly and allowed me to rub his head. He then started trying to take off my shoe. His mother 'Princess' kept a watchful eye on us all the time.

We re-entered the jungle with a ranger again in the after-
[illegible]n for feeding time. Orang-utans came through the trees from
[illegible] direction to get some bananas. The ranger knew each of
[illegible]y name and hollered out loudly to attract them. They
[illegible]unding through the trees from all sides. After a swim
[illegible]er we started our return journey back from Camp
[illegible]n the afternoon.

[illegible]ed about half-way back in another small ranger
[illegible]e tied up for the night. We all woke up early
[illegible]he cook chasing an orang-utan out of the tiny
[illegible]n of the boat. He was trying to steal some
[illegible] the early morning playing with a tame
[illegible]went off to witness another feeding ses-
[illegible] *Golden Apple* safe and sound that after-
[illegible]ill anchored in the same place and un-

[illegible] the local market at Kumai before
[illegible]n towards Singapore. There was
[illegible]e fresh bread and some vege-

utans seemed as interested in us as we were in them. They were unbelievably human-like. Their hands and ears are very similar to humans, and they ate their bananas just as you or I would. They were like extremely hairy ugly babies. The adults were about four feet high when they stood up vertically. 'Kosasai the king', who we saw on the second day, was the largest male in the park and much bigger and incredibly strong. Apparently he was attacked by a 4m crocodile a few years earlier and had killed it by breaking its neck.

We travelled upriver the first evening until about 8pm
off-load some supplies to Camp Leaky, the main camp
park. There are no roads in the entire park so everyt
be brought in by boat. It was dark before we f
some reeds for the night. After a dinner of
on our boat captain in a game of ches
hammered me. I think he greatly

The noise of insects and
ening. The mosquitoes w
repellents. They seer
legs were cover

The fol
in sear
in

m
sma
erupte
paths qui
new meanin

tables.

We crossed the equator for the second time on route to Singapore. We were back in the northern hemisphere after about nine months down under. I remembered the last time we had crossed the equator back in the Galapagos. Sitting on watch on my own under the dark skies gave me lots of time to think. I often thought of Dad. Memories of him had become much sweeter as time had passed and while sometimes it made me sad to think of him, most of time I remembered the good times and some of the stupid things he would say. It's the little things about people that I always tend to remember and cherish, the way they might laugh or do normal things differently, with Dad it was the same. He would have loved many of the places we had visited, especially the South Pacific. It was hard to imagine him not being around when we eventually managed to get home but that was something we would all have to deal with later. On the boat we would talk about him often. Something would come up in conversation and one of us would mention him. There were parts of him in each of us and I suppose these acted as cues and reminders.

The skyscraper sky-line of Singapore was a welcome relief from the relatively untamed Indonesia. As we passed through the Straits the shipping was intense. It was like trying to cross a dual-carriageway. The ships were the biggest we had ever seen, far larger than anything we had see in Panama, some of the oil tankers were well over a thousand feet long. We had to pass behind the stern of one to avoid the next one. They are deceptively fast and there was no way they could either stop or alter course in time to avoid us. We made it across safely and into the marina complex on the western side of Singapore.

Singapore was about as different from Indonesia as it could be. As the skyscrapers indicated to us coming in, it is a very modern city. Coming from the jungle it was great to get to

modern shops and bars again. Rebecca was delighted to get a chance to scout around the shops of which there are literally thousands of all types. Singapore has to be the cleanest, most organised, city in the world. Everything is spotless and no one ever seems to break any laws. For a start chewing-gum is not allowed to be chewed on the streets, smoking is prohibited in most restaurants and cafes and everyone obediently stands in taxi queues rather than hailing for one passing by. Laws are enforced in this country and you get a substantial fine if you break them so no one seems to. Not many Singaporeans own their own cars as the road tax is set deliberately high so as not to have too many cars on the road. Traffic congestion isn't a huge problem with thousands of people travelling to work every morning by the efficient underground metro system. Singapore is about the size of Munster with a population of over three million and at night the sky-line is incredible with its many beautifully lit skyscrapers.

It was here that we celebrated our one-year anniversary of being at sea. We went to an Indian restaurant that Tony insisted on, and the four of us burnt the hell out of our mouths on the unbelievably strong curry. Even Andy our 'in house' curry expert agreed that it was a little strong. We talked about the previous months and how much things had changed. We all missed Simon at different times and were worried about how his election campaign was going. We all knew he would be putting tremendous pressure on himself to succeed. Simon is a very proud person and for him, I knew, defeat would have been crushing, particularly in the circumstances. We had talked to Mum about how he was getting on in the campaign and she seemed confident he would do well.

It was a great day when we heard he had been elected. By all accounts it was an emotional day, with lots of Dad's friends there in support. For us, it was difficult to imagine the tension

and we all felt a little left out. We crowded around our satellite phone for news from Patrick. When I eventually managed to speak to Simon he was emotional about the whole thing and couldn't really speak. It was difficult for me to picture Simon as a TD, particularly when I remembered him on the boat slurping his cornflakes with Andy. At home it was all change.

We left Singapore on 30 October and headed north through the Malacca Straits towards Thailand.

10

Christmas Again

Thailand like Australia was going to be a long stop. We could not head across the Indian Ocean before the New Year on account of the monsoon season. We were all frustrated because we were going to have to wait until after Christmas. We had come so far at this stage that we really wanted to just keep going. Since we had returned back to the boat after Dad's death the trip had been different. I think all of us had, while enjoying ourselves, decided that it was something that had to be finished. Talk of home began to creep more and more into conversation. I think home was something that frightened us all to a degree. It's a horrible feeling knowing that things and people are changing without us being there to share in those changes. In many ways it felt as if we were in some sort of waiting period and that things couldn't be like they were when we returned. I suppose that is always a feature of extended travels.

We too were changing. The accumulative effect of our great loss and our unique experiences were bound to change us. There was a feeling that we would be somewhat different, to other people at least, by the time we made it home. Maybe I am being a little over analytical but I do think about these things quite a lot, and we really did have lots of time to contemplate such things. I don't think I had ever spent so much time on my own before and hours alone can play havoc with both the imagination and thoughts. For a couple of weeks we had all been very down, in fact, we had gone an entire day without speaking to each other. It wasn't that we were mad at each other or anything it was just that we had run out of things to

say. Two friends of mine had come and gone, they were both on their way to Australia for a year and it sounded so exciting as for us life was becoming very much the same. I know this may sound odd considering all the places we were visiting but it was just a bad time. People would come and go and then we would be left again just the four of us.

The King's Cup regatta in Phuket was a great break for all of us. The King's Cup is a sailing event held each year and boats from all over the world congregate to compete in Asia's premier regatta. For us it was a great chance to meet people our own age and in some ways to get a break from each other for a while. It was also, like the ARC race had been, a great chance to promote the Sail Chernobyl Project. We had been in contact with the organisers before we had arrived in Phuket and they seemed supportive. The King's Cup was a week-long event and on the Thursday we arranged to have a fundraising party for all the competitors. We also decided for the first time ever to race *Golden Apple* in the regatta. *Golden Apple* isn't a racing boat, she is very heavy and slow in comparison to more modern boats but we thought it would be a bit of fun to try.

Two days before the King's Cup began Andy was suffering from a tremendous pain in his ear. We had been very lucky up until now with illnesses or injuries. We were well equipped with medical supplies so we could deal with most things. Andy had tried a few of the pain-killers and general antibiotics to try and relieve the pain in his ear but nothing had worked so he decided to head to the local hospital in Phuket. Tony went with him for some moral support. This is how Andy described the experience: 'The hospital was remarkably modern and very clean and well run so I thought I was in for some great treatment. I sat in the doctor's chair totally relaxed. A Thai doctor (smelling of drink!) asked a few questions in his pidgin English and examined my good ear first. He decided to clean it out,

which involved poking it with some stainless steel apparatus, followed by some suction! Painful, but bearable. It's remarkable how sensitive the inside of your ear is.

'He then concentrated on my sore ear. First he poked his examining lens into my swollen ear, ooch! I expected a little sympathy. No chance, he set about torturing me for nearly twenty minutes. I can truly say it was the most painful experience of my life. I quickly became as white as a sheet, started sweating profusely, my eyes went watery, I became dizzy and I thought I was going to vomit with the pain. He continued to jab his iron utensil around my ear-drum with the delicacy of a butcher! I imagined myself as an SAS commando being interrogated by my captives. I was in a terrible state leaving the surgery. Tony quickly led me to a chair in the waiting-room. He's never seen me in such a terrible state.'

When Andy returned to the boat he could barely speak. The treatment did actually help, I just think that Andy had expected it to be a little more delicate.

The racing turned out to be a bit of a fiasco for us. I didn't mind too much that we weren't doing very well as I knew the boat wasn't really up to it. The others who had all been competitive racers before we left did find it a bit frustrating to see other boats just leaving us for dead, but after the first few days they too saw the funny side of it and we decided to not take it too seriously.

It was great to meet so many new people. There was an Irish boat competing and we became very friendly with the crew and shared a few long nights with them. They agreed to give us a hand with the fundraising party we had planned.

The Thursday night started as a complete disaster. The venue was a local bar and many of the people there had no interest in what we were trying to do. Phuket tends to attract some of the worst kind of people, I hate to generalise but many

of the men fall into the category of middle-aged Australian and American ex-pat losers living with beautiful Thai women. They are there because it is so cheap and their lifestyle can be relatively good. They have little concern for anything other than their own small world. Trying to convince these people of what we were trying to do turned out be a disaster. I gave a speech and absolutely no one was listening. One American said to Rebecca that he couldn't care if all the Russians burned in hell. Amid this we knew that it was going to be difficult, to say the least, to raise any money. A little despondent I asked Paddy, one of the Irish guys, if he had any ideas. It was then that he came up with the idea of a tug-of-war.

The tug-of-war was precisely what was needed to arouse interest. We were learning that most people don't really mind giving money to a charity if they are enjoying themselves. Often the cause, no matter how worthy, just won't interest people directly. The tug-of-war as a team event was well geared towards getting a crew from each of the boats. Before long we had over twenty teams battling it out. We, of course, entered ourselves but unfortunately were beaten by an English team in a tug that went on for over ten minutes, and despite completely biased refereeing by our Irish friends we just couldn't hold on. As the event went on the interest in Sail Chernobyl increased, we managed to sell over 200 T-shirts and got some great donations from many of the foreign boats. In the end we raised over £3,000. We also managed to get interviews with most of the sailing press and we all did an interview with the Asian equivalent of Sky Sports. So like both Las Palmas and Australia we had managed to spread the Chernobyl story around Asia.

We were all looking forward to Christmas in Malaysia, which was a month away. Mum and the others were coming out to join us and we couldn't wait to see them again. I was par-

ticularly eager to see Simon and I was anxious to see if becoming a Dáil deputy had changed him. Our spirits restored we headed back down to Langkawi, an island off Malaysia. In the week before the others were due to arrive out we once again set about doing a major overhaul of the boat. We cleaned and scrubbed *Golden Apple* until she looked like new. I knew Simon would be inspecting the boat looking for faults so I did not want to give him any excuses. He would enjoy comparing his reign as skipper with mine, not in a serious way but just your usual fraternal competition. We even got a few Christmas decorations and a little tree to brighten the place up. Malaysia being a Muslim country does not celebrate Christmas at all. They were in the middle of what they call Ramadan, which is a month-long fasting period. They couldn't pass anything between their lips during the daylight hours. They couldn't even swallow their own saliva. It was tremendously hot and many of them seemed dehydrated and were very sleepy looking. As Hinduism in Bali had shown me, the Muslim religion to an even greater degree was an example of the devotion of other religions. Muslim law here was far more pervasive than secular law. We would find this again later on as we entered the Middle East. It looked as if we would be the only ones celebrating Christmas.

◊

The website at this stage was very popular, particularly with schoolchildren, in Ireland. The schools' pack had been very well received by many schools and it was wonderful for us to receive so many messages to the boat. They were a real lift when we were feeling a bit down. This was one of our favourites:

Hello,

We are a small, three-teacher, primary school in Co. Offaly and we have been following the 'Sail Chernobyl' voyage over the last few months. We have written to them regularly and organised a sponsored penalty shoot-out and a fancy dress skipathon which has raised £656 to date. We use the internet a fair bit in the school as we are in an isolated rural setting and it brings the world right into our classroom. We have enjoyed following the Coveney trip hugely and will continue writing to them up until June.

Would there be any possibility that the crew would be able to visit us at some stage on their return? The children in the school have adopted them as the 'Coolest People on the Planet' and we think they are indeed worthy of that title. I'm sure a lot of schools write to the crew, but we have been following their adventures for so long that the children feel as if they know them. We would make them really welcome, even more so, maybe, than when the Liam McCarthy Cup came to the school recently, and believe me, that is saying something!

Thanks,

Catherine Doolan (Teacher) Lumcloon NS

I'm not sure about the title of 'coolest people on the planet', but messages like this did give us a feeling that what we were doing was making a difference. Lumcloon National School was in fact the only school we visited a week or so after we got home and we did get a wonderful reception.

This was our second Christmas away and our first without Dad. I didn't really know what form the others would be in when they arrived. Christmas was going to be one of those emotional hurdles we would all have to cope with. In many ways it was easier that we weren't at home but far away. We went to the airport on the twenty-second and it was great when the whole lot of them came bundling through the gate. They were all white-looking compared to us and came bearing gifts of all sorts. The four of us were surprised to see a big

metal lobster pot among the bags. While in Thailand Andy and Tony had made a lobster pot and had had no luck catching anything. One night we had left it outside a lobster hole but the pot was sabotaged by some night divers and all but destroyed. We had been explaining this lobster debacle in our website updates and a fisherman from Clonakilty in West Cork had read the messages and gave Mum what he called 'a good, honest to God Irish pot'. He said to her that he was sure it would tempt those foreign lobsters. Simon's present to Rebecca had to be the best. It was a cookie jar in the shape of a shark that made the sound of the *Jaws* music whenever the lid was lifted. When we were crossing the Atlantic Rebecca stole the last chocolate brownie, which happened to be his. There was war on the boat and she never heard the end of it. Something like a brownie tends to become very precious out in the middle of nowhere with nothing nice left to eat. Simon felt this new addition to the boat would be a safe place for the precious brownies.

New music was always a great tonic for the boat. The stereo was perhaps the most used piece of equipment on the boat. We had music playing for at least six or seven hours a day so you can imagine if we got some new CDs or tapes it made a great change. Thea and a good friend of mine used to send tapes of new music so at least I didn't lose an entire two years of current music. We got lots of the latest CDs from Pat and Emma and Simon for Christmas so we were delighted. We had some real rows on the boat over what music was played. Bec, Tony and I liked similar things, but unfortunately Andy and I clashed a bit over what was on. It had been worse when Simon was there because he liked the dreaded country music, which drove everyone mad.

Only Simon and myself stayed on the boat while the others spent Christmas in the hotel. The first night we didn't get to bed until at least four in the morning. He gave me a blow by blow

account of the election campaign and how it was to be a TD. I could remember the campaigns with Dad and it was hard to imagine Simon as the candidate. With Dave away in school Simon and Mum were the only ones at home and she had been a fantastic support to him, although it was difficult for her, during the election campaign. His relationship with Mum had changed greatly since we had seen him last. In fact it was one of the first things I noticed. It was clear they had grown very close over the past few months.

New Year's eve was a little sad although we all did our best to have a good time. It had been a real tough year for our family and we all hoped the year to come would be better. The farewells were once again difficult as the others headed off back home. Once again we were on our own and we had the Indian Ocean to cross.

11

Back to the Western World

After Christmas we were to spend very little time on land before we got home and with the exception of a two week stay in Malta we didn't stop for more than five days anywhere. The four of us had decided that we should be back before the schools in Ireland broke up for the summer holidays. Mimi had planned a day when all the schools that had been following us on the internet could come and see us and the boat. The date for our arrival home was set for 15 May. That gave us only five months to travel some 12,000 miles in a boat that could only average about 120 miles a day. We were in a rush.

The trip from Malaysia to Sri Lanka was about 1,000 miles. It was an uneventful crossing. The weather was perfect and we made good progress. We were all reading a tremendous amount. Books were becoming a wonderful escape for all of us. Some days while at sea the four of us would sit for hours, no one talking, all of us just reading, each of us engrossed in our own fictional world. For most of the second half of the voyage I was reading nearly three books a week. All types of books, whenever we got a chance to find a shop that sold English books we bought loads. We had also got into the routine of exchanging books with other boats, so we had a constant change of literature. I tried to read both light and heavy books as one was a relief from the other. I suppose it's like watching good and bad movies, sometimes I just didn't want thought-provoking books and was happy with a good detective story. I tried to avoid books about the sea or travelling in an effort to get my mind off what we were doing. Rebecca had finally begun to read *Lord of the Rings* and had become engrossed. The two of us discussed

Frodo's dilemmas in great detail much to the annoyance of the others. In fact the two of us tended to read more than the others and would spend hours discussing books we had both read. It was a great way of passing the time.

During these days at sea we also began to play games of various sorts. 'Trivial Pursuit' was a favourite although the version we had was old and most of the questions were out of date. Cards also became a feature of the days. I introduced poker and we played for various chores on the boat. The games became very heated, as only competition between brothers and sisters can be. One of the highlights was when we caught Tony cheating and he was forced to do both the wash-up and the worst watch.

Responding by email to the questions to the school kids also kept us busy. The questions varied from what it was like to sleep on a bed that was always moving, to what kind of music we liked, to if we'd do all this again? We took it in turn to answer the emails. I think the schools were amazed to get emails back directly from the boat. The technology was great – when we sent an email I was always astonished that they actually made it. On leaving our laptop computer it went via modem into our satellite telephone. From there it headed up to a satellite, back down into one of four Land Earth stations, back up to another communication satellite and from there into the terrestrial network in Ireland before popping up on the screen of a computer.

It may sound as if with all these things going on that we didn't do any sailing. The challenge of actually sailing the boat at this stage for us was not that great. I can remember Andy saying to me that what had been a bit of a let-down for him was that the sailing hadn't proved to be more difficult and more of a challenge. There was obviously always the uncertainty of the weather and maintenance but for ninety percent

of the time it took very little of our abilities to keep the boat going. A real challenge was to keep everyone motivated and happy and that is why we played these games and read so many books to keep our minds from going crazy. Sail Chernobyl was also proving a real challenge for us, and apart from the tangible difference we were making to the people of Belarus it also gave us a wonderful focus and sense of purpose.

Shortly after dawn on 20 January we arrived safely in Galle Harbour on the south coast of Sri Lanka. We were greeted almost immediately by the Sri Lankan navy who boarded us for an inspection before allowing us to moor in the harbour. The clearing in procedure here was one of the longest, it took the whole day. In the end I had to bribe the customs officials with a few boxes of cigarettes and a few beers just to get them off the boat.

Galle was a shock to us all, it was certainly the most underdeveloped place we had visited up until then. Many people don't wear shoes. Open sewage pipes run along the streets. Flies are everywhere covering the market and fish stalls, and the roads are absolutely lethal. We ventured into Galle town in one of the tuk-tuks, a three-wheeled open vehicle and their equivalent of a taxi, and missed lorries and buses by inches a number of times. We went to buy some fresh meat and we ended up witnessing the slaughter of an innocent chicken in front of our very eyes. I think Rebecca seriously considered becoming a vegetarian after the ordeal.

Our boat was anchored in the harbour where the Sri Lankan navy base is. At night these sailors were going around the harbour in a speed-boat dropping grenades into the water. There would be a huge bang and splash every time they went off. Sir Lanka has a political problem somewhat similar to Northern Ireland. The Tamil people, a small ethnic group with close ties in southern India, essentially want an independent

state. The navy base is a target for attacks. As soon as it gets dark and until morning the navy drop these grenades to guard ships from under-water rebel divers. We could feel the vibrations on our boat every time so as you can imagine we didn't sleep all that well.

We decided to head off on a tour of some of the sights and the three days we spent travelling around is something I will never forget – not because of the things we saw but because our driver was a complete lunatic. There were at least ten times where I thought this is it, we're dead, over-taking buses on hairpins with cliffs either side, missing bikes by inches and continuously on the wrong side of the road, if you could call them roads. I thought we had pot-holes in Ireland but they are merely little bumps compared to the huge craters on Sri Lankan roads. Poor Tony was in the front seat most of the time and I could see his face getting paler and paler as he gripped the seat.

Tony and I spent the whole of the second day arguing over tea production – something which neither of us had a clue about. I had told our driver to take it easy on the speed and the journey into the mountains was a little less nerve-wracking and we had some possibility of seeing something. It wasn't so much an argument as a long-winded discussion. Most of the tea in Sri Lanka is grown high up and always on a slope, so I assumed that these were vital factors in the production of tea. Tony maintained that the only reason that tea was grown in this way was because this was the only land they had. This went on for a few hours, much to the annoyance of Bec and Andy, each of us developing our rationale with absolutely no idea what we were talking about. Eventually we decided to ask an expert and stop at one of the many tea plantations. To the delight of the others I was completely wrong and had to endure another hour of Tony gloating over his victory. We had

these arguments from time to time. I had a similar one with Andy in Singapore regarding the speed at which the big container ships could unload and load up their new cargo, this one I had won. Andy and I had gone down to the maritime museum in the city to resolve the issue. We were all a little too proud to concede defeat in these ridiculous arguments.

The tea-pickers were amazing. They were all tiny women. Before coming to Sri Lanka I had no idea that all the tea was picked by hand. There were thousands of these little women scattered over the hills in among the little tea bushes that were up to their waists. They had baskets tied to their backs and their hands moved astonishingly quickly over the tea bushes to pick the ripe leaves and fill their baskets. In Sri Lanka nearly everyone drinks tea plain with no sugar or milk. Ever since our time there I have got into the habit of drinking tea that way. At home now, people find it strange when I drink tea just plain like that, particularly my mother who has been drinking tea with milk for years.

Kandy was an inland mountain town and, although still quite poor, it was more upmarket than Galle with a beautiful lake and Buddhist temple. It is in here that they keep, in a gold safe, a tooth from the first Buddha which is hundreds of years old and has been passed from temple to temple throughout the Buddhist world. From the temple we drove to the elephant orphanage nearby. Although Rebecca was a bit upset that we didn't get to feed the baby ones with bottles we did see over 50 of every size, age and shape kicking around happily in a river. It was in some ways like the orang-utan park in Borneo except with elephants. In Sri Lanka like Thailand the elephant is a sacred animal and treated, particularly by the older people, with great reverence. For us it was great to be able to get so near them and see so many together in as close to a wild environment as is possible.

We stayed overnight in the mountains in a guesthouse and spent most of the final day travelling back to Galle. It was here that for the first time in months, high up in the mountains, that we were freezing cold. We had been in the tropics for so long we had almost forgotten what it was like to be cold. The building was very old and had a fireplace in each of the rooms. Unfortunately the person running the place wouldn't give us enough wood to keep the fire going. I was staying in a room with Tony and we couldn't get to sleep because we were absolutely freezing. We both decided we had to find something to burn so I dismantled some of the boards underneath one of the spare beds. Tony coughed loudly to cover-up while I broke them so they would fit in the fire. It was clear that the people who were staying before us had done the same thing as the bed had only a few boards left. Soon we had a roaring fire and slept well.

Once we got back to the boat we quickly got ready to leave again, we were now heading for a new continent once again, Africa. We were heading for the former French colony of Djibouti at the southern end of the Red Sea. This was our second longest voyage of the trip some 2,000 miles across the Indian Ocean and we were all a little apprehensive. The longest was the transatlantic which took us nineteen days and this trip was going to take in or around fifteen days. We never really talked about the length of our voyages as the best thing to do was to try and forget about arriving and just take one day at a time; get into a routine so to speak. We would drive ourselves mad thinking about not being able to go for a walk or meeting new people or just getting away from each other for a few hours.

We left Galle harbour shortly after noon. I had the usual dramas with the customs and immigration officials, which took the whole morning. Tony and Bec went off to do the shopping and Andy filled the boat up with fuel.

Getting news from home was always great and reminded us about what other people were doing. The BBC world service is a wonderful way to keep in touch with what is going on around the world and more specifically back in the British Isles and Ireland. Sometimes the reception wouldn't be great but most of the time we could pick it up pretty clearly on our long-range radio. On this trip we all huddled around the radio to listen for the latest news on the Ireland–Wales rugby match. While the reception crackled we still managed to get some of the atmosphere of the great win. Of course it wasn't the same as watching it on television but we did jump around like idiots, and scream 'Come on Ireland' a few times out there in the middle of nowhere.

One of the strange things about the very long voyages is that it becomes difficult to know what time it is. The clock didn't really mean anything as we were constantly moving. We tended to try and structure our days around the sun. It is bizarre to be able to choose what time you want it to be and not knowing for certain what time it actually is, at least on our watches anyway. The other thing was that it didn't really matter what time it was. Time was something we had lots of and it was better not to worry about what time it was. We just kept sailing through miles and miles of ocean

We had our first medical drama during this long trip. One of the winches slipped while Tony was adjusting the sails and the handle smashed him on the arm cutting him quite badly. Rebecca with her limited medical training was required to put in the necessary three stitches. As I said at the beginning both Rebecca and Tony did a medical course before we left where they practised stitching on pigs' trotters, but as Rebecca said it is a little different when it's your brother. Anyway she did a great job and the wound healed up in a few days. Tony was a little shook-up despite being a great patient, considering his

doctor. We gave him some antibiotics just in case infection might develop. He was lucky that it wasn't more serious and he didn't break a bone. It brought it home to us that while things were all going smoothly, how very suddenly they could go wrong.

As with South America, Africa conjured up images from what I had seen on television or read about. Before we arrived I thought of great big plains with high yellow grass and lions with brown manes and golden backs roaming like kings, sunsets that melted shimmering and silhouetting the tall monkey trees with their little leafy canopies and giraffes galloping. At the same time I thought of tremendous poverty and starvation, small children and old people with swollen stomachs and flies around their watery empty eyes. These pictures of beauty and desperation beat around in my head so in the end I didn't know what to expect from our glimpse of this massive continent.

Djibouti turned out to be as grim a place as there could be. It combined much of what is so terribly wrong about the world in which we live. I had been prepared to see extreme suffering, like it had been in Belarus, but it is very different to see and hear and smell human decay. We had been to many poor places on this voyage but nothing quite came near the levels of suffering, poverty, squalor and hopelessness of this place.

Andy and I went for a wander around the town. We needed to buy a few specific things for the boat, but we also wanted to see what the place was really like. We found young children dressed in rags with no shoes, begging on every street. People lay asleep in shaded doorways. Miserable shanty towns made from cardboard and corrugated iron spread into the suburbs. Goats wandered freely around the streets and pathetic looking donkeys struggled to pull small carts into the filthy marketplace. As we walked through the market, people were swooshing flies from their eyes, and searching through the rubbish skips

for food or anything that might be of some use. These people appear to lack hope. Every day is a battle for survival. The two of us were truly depressed when we returned to the safe sanctuary of the boat anchored off the shore. I wondered if all of Africa was as bad as this, or perhaps worse.

There is still a big French presence here. There is an army base and the infamous Foreign Legion has a training camp and the port was full of military ships. There are a few modern bars and restaurants in the town which are generally full of the French soldiers and their families and friends. Although the French officially left twenty-two years ago, the ridiculously high prices still remain, making it even more expensive than Paris.

We were in one of the bars watching the Wales versus France rugby match surrounded by French soldiers when one of the soldiers asked me if I was Irish. He was wearing the complete uniform of khaki shorts, the white cylindrical peaked hat, long socks and khaki shirt. His accent was clearly Irish and I told him I was from Cork. It turned out that he was from Drogheda and had spent the previous 15 months in the Foreign Legion in Djibouti. After a couple of drinks I asked him what it was like to be in reputedly the toughest army in the world. He said they trained very hard, each morning they ran twenty or so miles before breakfast and then they did manoeuvres and more combat-training. He told me of a recent mission they had been on in central Africa where the vehicle they were in was attacked by local rebels. The commander of the group of six of them completely lost his cool and they started to retaliate with machine-gun fire of their own killing over thirty people, civilians as well as rebels. I must say it was a little unnerving talking to someone who had mowed down lots of people with a machine-gun. He talked so matter-of-factly about this sort of thing as if it was like any other job. He was delighted to meet other Irish people and introduced us to

a few of the other legionnaries including another Irishman from Kerry. They showed us around the seedy underworld that was Djibouti by night. The four of us felt safe with our new Irish friend and his group – it was reassuring knowing that if we were to get into any trouble that we had a couple of well-trained psychos with us.

The day before we were due to leave for Suez we couldn't believe it when *Madjik* arrived into the harbour. It was like Darwin all over again. They always seemed to arrive the day before we were due to leave. Since we had last seen them in Bali we hadn't heard from them. They had been home in America for Christmas and when we left Thailand without hearing from them we assumed we would never see them again. Mike told me that they had seen the name *Golden Apple* on the immigration records in Galle in Sri Lanka and knew we couldn't be too far ahead. It was great to see them again. The three kids were full of news from home. Mike had sorted out some of business problems that had been worrying him. Mike and Amy are your classic American success story. The two of them had bought a bar in their early twenties and had worked incredibly hard over the next ten years and now owned four bars and two hotels and lots of property around the Michigan area. They had employed managers to run their businesses, bought a boat and decided to sail around the world. Mike was always hatching new business plans, which he would discuss with me. We had become good friends with them and we vowed once we got to Suez to go into Cairo together and explore the pyramids and sights.

Before we headed off we had to fill the boat up with fuel and this turned out to be a real debacle. We brought in our six jerry cans to the petrol station near the dock, with the simple ambition of filling them and paying and leaving. The filling started out reasonably well with me explaining what I wanted

in my poor schoolboy French to the yellow-toothed fuel man. When the cans were full, one of the pump attendants for some reason failed to see the amount on the dial before filling the Isuzu Trooper that had just arrived. This caused uproar with his boss, the yellow-toothed man, as he then didn't know how much fuel we had taken despite the fact that the amounts of each can are clearly labelled. He failed to understand that the cans quite clearly (to me anyway) added up to 175 litres. Despite my protestations and frantic French arm-waving he proceeded to pour all 175 litres back into the main tank and re-pump it through the sacred gauge into our clearly marked cans and all this took about three hours. All Andy and I could do was laugh at the stupidity of it all, having given up the notion that getting annoyed would make any difference.

The most difficult sailing of the trip was from the time we left Djibouti until we got to Malta. We had always known that the Red Sea leg was going to be our most difficult. The wind here nearly always blows strongly from the north, which makes it very difficult to make good progress towards the Suez Canal. We didn't have time to take it slowly and hop up along the coast so we just had to push on up the middle. The countries on either side of the Red Sea are not the most hospitable, Saudi Arabia was on the eastern side and they are very unwelcoming to any boats and a few weeks previously a boat had been attacked and robbed on the Ethiopian side.

We were lucky for the first four days of the trip as we got winds from the south, which brought us up about half-way towards Suez. I was shocked to see gunfire in the night sky as we passed by the northern coast of Yemen. It was scary to see all these little orange streaks flying across the sky about ten miles to the west of us. We didn't have any idea what was going on and were relieved when we had passed. Our friends in *Madjik* had seen the gunfire as well and were a little con-

cerned when we talked to them on the radio. It was nice having another boat near us, we talked all the time about changes in the weather. We even helped finalise a business deal for Mike using our satellite phone to answer a call from his accountant in America and then sent on the relevant information using the radio. It brought international business to a slightly ridiculous level.

After the four days of favourable winds we got complete calms for nearly two days and had to use the engine. Andy took advantage of the good weather to test his skills with the sextant. For those of you who don't know what a sextant is, it is a device used for plotting your position. Knowing where you are at a given time is the most important thing in navigation – it was a problem that puzzled sailors for hundreds of years. Ordinarily we got our position from our GPS or global positioning system, a small computer device that uses satellites to determine our exact position. Before the advent of satellite technology the sextant was the only way to navigate offshore, and nowadays the skill of using the sextant is rare among mariners. I am not going to go into the complicated mathematics of how the position is determined using the sextant, but basically by pointing the sextant at the sun at given times of the day it was possible to calculate where we were. Andy was determined to figure it out, we had been given a loan of the sextant for the trip from an old friend of the family and Andy said there was no way he could face him if he hadn't at least tried to use it. After a whole day and pages of sums Andy emerged with a big grin, he was delighted with himself, he had managed to determine our position accurate to one mile.

By the fifth day the bread had gone mouldy and the wind had turned into the north and strengthened. These two things quite obviously weren't connected but they were the things that concerned us. We all loved bread and it was a nightmare

when it started to go, Andy and I usually continued to eat it by just cutting off the mouldy corners and toasting the hell out of it under our little grill. The bread that Tony made wasn't great really. We did our best to encourage him but unfortunately the bread usually turned out to be very chewy and difficult to swallow. I think the problem was that the oven wasn't hot enough to get it to rise.

The conditions deteriorated considerably on the night of the fifth day. It was on this night that we had our first real drama of the voyage, I think it was the only time that I thought things might go seriously wrong. As the seas got very big and steep and the wind very strong the boat was pounding into the waves. With all the banging we must have damaged some of the caulking in between the planks on the bottom of the boat and had sprung a serious leak. We were taking in a lot of water and the bilge and engine room were fast becoming flooded. Ordinarily this wouldn't be too much of a problem as when too much water comes in we simply pump it out with the bilge pumps. These pumps are located under the floor-boards and just pump out the water when switched on. However on this night the pumps failed, the water level got very high and the floor-boards started to float around. We simply had to get the pumps working. It was about 2am and for two hours I was in the engine room, with about 4 feet of headroom being thrown around in the waves, knee deep in oily water, crouched over, dismantling and fixing the pump. In the end I managed to fix it but not without lots of cursing and tools flying everywhere. Just as the water problem seemed to be resolved the wind began to pick up even further to about 45 knots and our mainsail ripped in half. It was a very old sail and the stress just became a little too much for it. All of us were up on deck with the waves washing over us and we frantically pulled down the sail – by then we were all exhausted but relieved that we had

managed to deal with the dramas.

When the weather got like this it became almost impossible to do anything. Everything is being thrown around, cooking and eating become a real battle but going to the toilet is probably the most difficult thing. Managing to land your backside anywhere near the toilet seat becomes almost impossible, and staying on is like balancing an egg on a plate of wobbling jelly. As you can imagine we were looking forward to getting in if for nothing else but to go to the toilet in peace, poor Tony hadn't been for the previous three days.

After three more days of frustrating sailing, making very slow progress we finally entered the Gulf of Suez. It was a sad time for all of us and one we wished we were at home for. It was a year since Dad had died. It was hard for us to imagine him not being around, and not being at home. It was something we hadn't really had to get used to. As we got closer and closer to home, I thought of him more and more. I knew the fact that he would not be there when we came in was going to take away from the whole undertaking for me. He had been looking forward to it so much. Living at home without him around was something I was worried about – these were bridges to be crossed when we arrived home. Mum had decided at the last minute to join us in Cairo and do the trip with us to Malta – to be with us for Easter – so we were all really looking forward to seeing her.

Mike, Amy and the kids had found the Red Sea as draining as we did. They were a day behind us arriving into Port Suez and were relieved to have finished with the Red Sea. The port of Suez is where the canal begins and like in Panama there were many ships anchored in the harbour waiting for their transit.

Egypt was our first and only stop in the Middle East and the Arab world is indeed a truly different sort of place. For a

start they write here from right to left and not the other way around like us and the alphabet is entirely different. This made finding any shops or supplies very difficult as we literally had no clue what any signs or words meant. It was incredibly dry. Everywhere there was a dust that blew up with the strong winds and covered everything with a thin film. The desert came right down to the sea. The rolling dunes of reddish sand stretching back as far as we could see contrasted sharply with the blue sea. Most of the buildings were themselves a sandy colour and were quite dilapidated looking. In the morning we were woken to the Muslim wailing which was blasted out on loud-speaker from the main mosque. As with Malaysia, Egypt was fundamentally Muslim and it was almost impossible for us to get a drink anywhere. It's not like we were raving alcoholics but at the same time after the long journey up the Red Sea we would have liked a few beers. We did manage to find a small sort of back road speak-easy where the barman reluctantly gave us a few beers. It was like something out of prohibition America. A few people from other boats came with us and between the ten of us we cleaned the bar out – only having two beers each. The barman couldn't understand that one beer per person just wasn't enough.

Cairo was a truly amazing place. It was a two and a half hour drive through the dusty and dry desert from the port of Suez. We had gone by bus with Mike and his family and met up with Mum at the airport. It was great to see her and from the moment we met her she was tremendously enthusiastic about being in one of the most historic cities in the world and couldn't wait to get going. She was, and still is, studying history in university as a mature student and to come to arguably the most historical city in the world, which she had only read about in books, was something she was really looking forward to. She spent the journey in the bus back to the hotel pointing

out in her guide book the various places we should visit.

Cairo has a population of over twenty million and the traffic was unbelievable. The sound of car-horns and yelling was almost deafening. There didn't appear to be any system as to who had right of way and poor Mum was a nervous wreck as our daring driver wended his way through the traffic. It wasn't as scary for us having been through the complete Sri Lankan rally experience during our tour there.

Our first stop was the Egyptian National Museum. There were many fantastic things in this wonderful museum; it was hard to believe that some of the artifacts dated back nearly five thousand years. Of all the exhibits, for me the most special was that of the Queen Nefertiti. Though not as famous or as striking as the golden exhibit of Tutenkamen, the story of this stunning queen was fascinating. Very little is known of Nefertiti, and to this day no one can say exactly who she was. She wasn't of royal lineage and some believe that she wasn't even Egyptian. There is a coloured bust of her now in Berlin, which shows the rosy tint of her complexion and suggests that she may have been of northern stock. Most of the statues, drawings and carvings of ancient Egypt were, while beautiful, stilted and seemed to me at least to lack emotion. Nefertiti was different and the depictions of her and her husband Akhenaten are warm and very loving. There is a wonderful limestone tablet of her sitting on her husband's knee, which was a radical departure in the art of this time. It was nice to know that these people did seem to have a bit of fun, and weren't just beautiful and powerful monarchs who never laughed.

The Pyramids were as impressive as I had hoped they would be, standing huge against the blue sky, proud and defiant. It was hard to imagine what they would have been like when this massive city wasn't circling them. We spent the day there, Andy, Tony and Bec along with the crew of *Madjk* went

on a camel ride up around the Pyramids. Mum and I walked instead, I am not all that fond of camels or horses, so I was relieved when Mum said she would prefer to walk. We went into the middle of the Great Pyramid, which is the biggest of the three at the Giza site. The tunnel led to a small central tomb, which was a little disappointing considering how massive the construction was on the outside. We stayed in and around the Pyramids until nightfall and it was great to see the sun set behind these amazing wonders of the world. At night they look more impressive than during the day. They are wonderfully lit and the laser show depicting the history of the Pharaohs was a spectacular mixture of modern technology and an ancient and wonderful world.

The Citadel was the old town of Cairo, lying high on a hill overlooking the city. Inside the walls of this fortified town is one of the largest and oldest mosques of the Arab world. I had never really had the opportunity to meet many Muslims in Ireland, and like many Irish people I suppose I was somewhat wary of a religion that seemed so fundamentalist and strict. Like I have already mentioned with regard to the Muslim and Buddhist religions in Malaysia and Thailand, the commitment of the people to their faiths astounded me. So much of what we see and know regarding the Arab world comes through the media and it seems to present a very one-sided and negative view. The guide we met in the Citadel was the first time I had spoken to a Muslim about his faith and what it meant. He explained carefully, and with great colour, the history behind his beliefs and in the space of about two hours while not exactly converted, I did at least have some small understanding and respect for what is one of the most influential doctrines in the world. At its heart, like nearly all creeds, Islam is based on essential goodness, but sadly like most religions, and unlike our guide, it has been warped by its zealots. After the Citadel we

made our way back to Suez to rejoin the boat.

The following day in Suez Mum, Bec and I went to the market to stock up for the trip to Malta. It was an experience that the three of us will never forget. It was a little like it had been in Sri Lanka. The market sold every type of animal alive or dead. As far as we could see there wasn't really any widespread refrigeration in Suez so meat of any type was slaughtered in front of you or you bought it alive. There was no such thing as a conventional supermarket. Women with ten or fifteen live chickens hanging off each arm hassled us to buy them. Little rabbits were crammed into cages and were bought by the dozen for making stews. The beef was horrible looking, they seem to eat every part of the cow here, from the heads to the skins to the eyes. As we passed through the market we watched beef being unloaded from the back of a truck by men with no shirts, carrying the carcasses on their shoulders and over their heads, with the blood and innards dripping down their backs. The whole thing was disgusting for us, Bec and Mum felt a little ill and as soon as we had got what we needed we headed off back to the boat.

Our crossing through the Suez Canal wasn't really as exciting as the Panama Canal, given there were no locks. It is like a giant ditch cutting some 160km through the desert. We had two pilots with us for the trip, one for the first day and a different one for the second. Asrof our first pilot was a very decent fellow. He was young and very well-mannered and despite what we had read in all the guide books didn't look for much in the way of a tip or bribe. He quietly took out his mat, took off his shoes, washed his feet and hands four times during the day and faced Mecca to kneel and pray on the deck. He wasn't in any way pious or self-conscious about it, he just got on with it. The pilot on the second day was a much different story. He did look like some Middle Eastern gangster in a James Bond

film. He was older, short and fat, his hair was greased back over the collar of his gaudy fake leather jacket. He wore sunglasses that covered his eyes and his dark face and refused to talk to us despite speaking perfect English. We were all relieved to have him off when we got to Port Said on the Mediterranean side of the canal. He had scoured the boat for things we might give him, cigarettes, food, money, beer, anything. In the end I had to literally tell him to get the f**k off our boat.

We said our farewells for the last time to Mike and Amy and their kids once we got to Port Said. They were heading north towards Israel while we were heading west to Malta. We were not going to see them again on the trip so we had a farewell dinner for them on our boat. Tony as usual cooked a great meal and we agreed to stay in touch through email over the next few months and in the future. We had all grown to be good friends and we gave the three kids Sail Chernobyl T-shirts to remember us. Unfortunately the smallest T-shirt was miles to big for little Keegan but he reckoned he would grow into it. It was the same when I had teased him about the size of his ears, he had said that he would grow into them.

It was as great a feeling when we had reached the Mediterranean as it had been when we came through the canal in Panama and into the Pacific. We all felt we were almost home. We were back in European waters for the first time in 14 months. We quickly set sail for Malta with the aim of getting there before Easter.

We had a very fast and adventurous first twenty-four hours, with a gale blowing us at tremendous speeds from behind. Unfortunately these strong winds veered around to the west, so progress became very slow and uncomfortable much like the Red Sea. Mum was holding up well to her first real rough passage. She had been out with us in the South Pacific but this was different. It was very cold at night and we were back to the oil-

skins and boots again. With the strong westerly winds against us, we had been unable to make much headway towards Malta. We thought about trying to stop in Crete for a day or two on the way but unfortunately we couldn't find a suitable harbour. A little down, we pushed on to Malta passing along the south coast of Crete with its high mountains still tipped with white and the terracotta roofs of houses in clusters lower down by the inhospitable coast.

As we cleared the coast of Crete we began to see many military aircraft on their way to the Balkans. We had been following the news on the BBC world service and knew the situation had escalated into the bombing campaign. Luckily we were far enough south not to be in any direct danger but it was a little eerie to see the big bombers. I thought of our friends back in Djibouti – maybe they had been drafted in. As we approached Malta we encountered a few American and British navy ships heading for the Adriatic. We kept on sailing, pushing west towards Malta. If someone asked me what direction I was heading during the past two months I could have answered like a cowboy in an old western, 'I'm going west, goddammit, I'm going west'.

12

'Golden Apple, Golden Apple, this is Cork Harbour Radio'

We arrived into the old harbour in Valletta on the island of Malta at dusk on Good Friday. We were all tired and really looking forward to a rest and a chance to meet some people of our own age who spoke English. In just over two months we had travelled from Thailand to Malta and the journey, with very little time on land, had taken its toll on us and the boat. This famous old harbour looked fantastic as the sun disappeared, the tall bastions that led down to the sea were lit by an orangy white and the reflection of the white cross on St John's cathedral shimmered on the surface of the calm navy water.

We tied to the quay wall on Manoel Island, the small island lying on the western side of the old city of Valletta. It was a relief to be tied to the land and have as much of both electricity and water as we wanted. The boat needed a real wash, it was still covered in salt and dust from the journey through the Red Sea and Suez. To be honest we too needed a wash. I think Bec was delighted to be able to have as many, and as long, showers as she wanted without me giving out to her about how much water she was using.

On Easter Saturday we went to St John's cathedral for the Easter ecumenical service. Mum was determined that we go to mass, we hadn't been in months and she felt we could all do with a little spirituality. It turned out to be a spectacular night. The simple, sober façade of St John's gives no clue of its magnificently decorated interior. The cathedral was built between 1572–1581 as a conventional church for the Order of St John

and the knights spent a small fortune embellishing the interior. The ceiling is similar to the Sistine chapel. It is painted in oils and depicts a narrative of the life of St John the Baptist. The walls are adorned with massive tapestries and each of the small chapels off the main church carry wonderful paintings including a Caravaggio. For me the floor was most impressive. There are over two hundred knights buried under the floor and the pavimento (floor paving) consists of numerous multi-coloured marble tombstones bearing, along with carvings of skeletons and symbols of death, the names and escutcheons of past members of the order.

The service began in complete darkness with each member of the congregation holding a candle, gradually as the service progressed the church became brighter and brighter, in keeping with the Resurrection, revealing the beauty of this extraordinary building. In the middle of this Tony and myself somewhat irreverently got a desperate dose of the giggles. We had both spotted, at the same time, across the aisle a woman who looked the image of Peter Clohessy the Irish rugby international. She kept staring malevolently at us. The two of us, like kids, just couldn't stop laughing until Mum who also found it somewhat amusing told us to cop on.

While St John's cathedral in itself was amazing, the story of the knights themselves, and particularly the Great Siege of Malta, is truly incredible. Most wars in history, and indeed today, were fought along a religious or ethnic axis. The great siege of Malta was one of the most remarkable military showdowns between Christians and Muslims. In 1565 the Knights of St John with some 9,000 men defended the tiny island of Malta against a Turkish force of 40,000 men and 180 ships. The battle was a fierce one but the knights held out and recorded a remarkable victory. It was a triumph for courage and bravery against terrible odds. I don't mean this to be a history lesson but both

Cairo and Malta are spectacular for their rich history and to be in places of such vivid historical reminders was a real window into the past. To stand on the ramparts where boiling oil was poured mercilessly on the advancing Turks or watch the sun set behind the Great Pyramids or marvel at the beauty of a painted ceiling gave me a real sense of the savagery, ingenuity and beauty of our ancestors that is still so relevant today.

We began preparing for our last fundraising party and we were lucky here to have the help of the Irish consulate. Tony Cassar, the Irish consul, was a keen sailor and he was very enthusiastic to help with the venue, guest list and refreshments. He also had some good contacts in the media, which resulted in a couple of newspaper articles and two television interviews. We had lots of visitors down to the boat and they were very interested in what we were doing. We also managed to organise an account with a Maltese bank so that it would be easier for people to give donations. It had been a big problem particularly in Australia, and people simply were not prepared to send cheques to an Irish bank account. We hoped that the local bank account would help in Malta . The party was set for the day before we were due to head off for Gibraltar – 16 April.

We met some wonderful people in Malta. We were lucky that we had some contacts to call on when we got here. A close friend of the family and his wife keep their boat in Malta and they came out to see us. They were very generous and helped us get things organised for the boat. They also asked their many Maltese friends to look after us so we made some great friends in our two weeks there and it turned out to be one of our most enjoyable stops. Malta is quite a small place so I think we were a bit of a novelty. The lads even got roped in to a local rugby match. They played well despite not having played in nearly two years. The highlight for Bec and I, who went to watch, was the female streakers who ran on midway through the second

half and mauled an exhausted and bewildered Andy.

The fundraising party turned out to be a great success. It was held in the beautiful Royal Malta Yacht Club overlooking the harbour. We had moved *Golden Apple* up in front of the club so everyone could see the type of boat in which we had travelled so far. It was a little more formal than the events we had held in other countries. Tony Cassar, the Irish consul, spoke about what we were doing and I responded by trying to give a feel for what life was like for the people of Belarus. I think everyone was touched by the photographs and slides we displayed and what I had said as we made over £3,000 on the night. The evening reminded me of that Ferro Rocher advertisement and I was waiting for one of the aristocratic women to say to Tony Cassar – 'Ambassador you are spoiling us'.

In the middle of the party we had a real drama and Andy and myself had to perform almost James Bond type heroics to save our boat from dragging its anchor onto the rocks. The evening had been calm but we were a little bit nervous about anchoring the boat in front of the club because it was very deep and reputedly had poor holding. Suddenly a strong gust of wind whistled through the harbour and the boat started drifting pretty fast towards the rocky shore. We were talking to one of the guests when someone shouted that the boat was moving. The two of us raced down the hill from the yacht club to our little dinghy and sped out to the boat. After a little panic we managed to get the anchor up and move the boat to safety. When we got back to the party most of the people had left and the barman jokingly accused us of creating all the drama for effect.

◊

Mum flew home the following morning relieved we were

going to be back in Ireland soon and that afternoon we set sail for Gibraltar. It was another 1,000 mile trip. After the first two days of heavy weather much like it had been in the Red Sea we got flat calms for most of the way to Gibraltar. We had to use the engine and a day out from Gibraltar we were running very low on fuel. We were forced to pull into the south coast of Spain to a port called Benalmadena in the middle of the night and wait until the morning to refuel before setting off again for Gibraltar. It took us nearly eight hours to cover the last ten miles with wind and strong current against us. We had a debate on board about when we should use our last few precious litres of fuel. We just had enough litres to manoeuvre into the fuel dock. We were terrified we'd be stranded in the middle of the shipping lanes with no fuel and no wind. I wouldn't mention this stop but for the great night we had there with four golfers from Athlone. We were all stressed when we finally made it in to the tricky harbour, so I suggested we head up to the town and try and find a bar to have a few beers and relax before going to bed. We found a bar called the Dutch Inn. Despite its name it was in fact an Irish bar and we got chatting to the owner who was originally from Dublin. It was then that these four Irish guys arrived. They had heard about us at home and refused to allow us buy a drink. One of them had only one arm which was quite remarkable considering he was on a golfing trip. We sang Irish songs late into the night and Bec took them all on on the dance floor. It was great for us to get a taste of Irish humour again after so long, it gave us a yearning for home – and we weren't far away now.

The rock of Gibraltar looked incredible from the sea as we approached the harbour on the evening of 26 April. The tall cliffs were dramatically lit up and the buildings looked incredibly crammed onto the small colony. We moored right next to the airport runway, so there was a tremendous sound when-

ever a plane landed only a 100 yards away. Gibraltar is technically part of Britain and it feels that way walking down the main street. Everywhere there are British shops, Tescos, Sainsburys and the pubs are called the traditional Red Lion and Corner House. It was a strange sort of place, there was clearly an antagonistic feeling from the Spanish towards the people of the colony and likewise from the colonials towards the Spanish. A few friends of mine who were on holidays in the south of Spain called down to say hello and bring me out for a night. The car had Spanish registration plates and as we drove through one of the streets we got attacked with eggs. Unfortunately I had the window down and got an egg in the window – the car was literally covered in egg. It was another one of those bizarre incidents of this whole trip but we did see the funny side of it and were impressed by the accuracy of the throw, which as far as we could see came from the window of an apartment block.

We only stayed two days in Gibraltar as time was fast running out. A big reception had been planned for 15 May and we simply couldn't be late. We were told by Mimi that the schools' website project had really taken off and that there were over 2,000 people a day logging on to the site. She told us that the interest in the whole project had become huge and that there were going to be hundreds of people there to welcome us in. We didn't really believe her as we felt she always tended to be over-optimistic. I suppose we all hoped there would be a good reception for us, but didn't really have any idea what to expect. We were all tremendously excited.

So we were off again. We were heading for Bayona. This was our first stop way back at the beginning of the voyage. Technically this was going to be where we completed our circumnavigation. It took us a whole day to pass through the Straits of Gibraltar with a strong current and wind against us, but once through we found favourable winds and made good

progress north towards Bayona. We had an extra crew member for this leg, Andy, a friend from England. He had never really sailed before so he didn't really know what he was getting himself into but he was very excited and enthusiastic. He was tremendously interested in how everything worked and for us it was good to demonstrate it to him. We had become so familiar with how things worked that to explain it to someone new to sailing was refreshing.

We arrived into Bayona in the early hours of 2 May and sailing in, early Sunday morning, brought a few tears to our eyes. It is the first place we've been to twice and I suppose we felt a certain sense of achievement completing the circumnavigation. We spoke to Simon that day and he seemed emotional as the last time we were in Bayona he was actually skipper. That seemed a lifetime ago. We went out to celebrate on Sunday night and also to let off a bit of steam after our five days at sea.

It was back to work for us all as we all wanted *Golden Apple* to be looking her best for our arrival in Cork. Tony and Bec made a start on the varnish work while Andy and I struggled around in the dirty engine room changing belts and filters and just generally trying to tidy up that part of the boat.

We became quite friendly with people from other boats on the marina. The French people on the boat next to us had a remarkable story to tell. The boat was based in La Rochelle and two men bring three children for two months, every two months, on a trip on this boat. It is a rehabilitation programme set up to help young offenders or kids from troubled homes and families. The aim is to help put them on the straight and narrow and at the same time mix with people who have similar problems. One of the men in charge acts as a father or guardian to them and the other is the skipper of the boat. Looking and talking to the kids it seemed like a great project.

Bayona was a real time for reminiscing about the previous months at sea. We were nearly home and yet we still had another week before we were going to be back. I can remember us sitting in the bar talking away about the trip when we got onto the topic of 'what if a film were ever made of this whole thing' who would play the various roles. None of us could really think of any one that we thought suited the parts. Tony eventually came up with what was typical of his humour, he suggested that Samuel L. Jackson play him. The four of us just couldn't stop laughing for about half an hour. We never really got on to who would play the rest of us.

We could finally see the coast of Cork. It was a grey morning and cold. The wind had picked up a bit so we were under full sail, and heeled over nicely. We had made great progress from Bayona and were all relieved that the Bay of Biscay had not hammered us again. We were all terribly excited, none of us had really slept at all as we were all a little nervous about what to expect. Days like these often turn out to be an anti-climax. It's not that I ever had a day like this before in my life but at the same time I had had some big days before and they had always tended to disappoint. Rebecca spent nearly an hour getting herself ready, she was determined not to look and smell like some old sea dog, so she showered and washed and painted her finger-nails. She looked great when she came up on deck and I gave her a cup of tea to calm her down a little. Us lads had planned on looking as sea doggy as possible with beards and salty hair. Tony in particular fancied the old sea dog look but in the end we too had a shower and shaved. Finally we caught sight of Roches Point lighthouse and we all got a little teary.

Way back when we were flying back to the boat in Tahiti Tony had bought a tape of the greatest hits of Frank Sinatra. We had all loved the music and after about a week of playing it

non-stop I decided that it should be the music we played when we saw the white paint of Roches Point lighthouse. I know it might sound sort of nostalgic and dramatic but for us at the time it was very genuine. After those first few bars of 'My Way' we were all crying like blubbering fools.

I had known for a while that it was going to be an emotional day when we got back. For us there was a huge sense of achievement, a sort of inner belief that we had done something quite unique and special. It was hard for us to believe that we had gone the whole way around the world, but when we saw Roches Point it hit home. It had been a roller-coaster ride of emotions for all of us that I think it was going to take some time to settle down. We had been through an awful lot together and it was difficult to think that the special bond, which we had forged through a huge variety of experiences, was soon going to be broken. While obviously we would always be brothers and sister we were never going to be as close again. Dad was on all our minds, this was a day that he would have loved and one when he would have been very proud. We had tried to put it out of our minds but seeing the very cliffs and water where he had fallen brought it all rushing back.

◊

'*Golden Apple, Golden Apple,* this is Cork Harbour Radio, do you read over'.

'Cork Harbour Radio, this is *Golden Apple* I read you clearly over'.

'*Golden Apple* we would like to welcome you all home and well done'.

It was great to hear a Cork voice on the radio, it had been so long and I was so used to hearing foreign voices that I got a bit of a fright. Simon, Patrick, Adi Roche and a few other friends arrived out on the Irish navy ship the *Aisling*. We met them at

the entrance to the harbour and they escorted us in. We were flattered that they had offered to do it, it was a real honour for us. Pat and Simon were waving madly and were as excited as we were to see *Golden Apple* finally home.

As we passed in through the entrance of the harbour loads of boats came out to welcome us, boats of all shapes and sizes carrying all sorts of people. We couldn't believe that so many people cared so much to come out and see us. Two helicopters appeared which was incredible and we were told they were filming for RTE. As we came around the corner passed Currabiny pier we could see a massive crowd of people along the road in Crosshaven and at the yacht club. We were very humbled and overwhelmed by the crowds. We slowly motored up the river joking with friends in the other boats as we passed. We were all really looking forward to meeting Mum who was on one of the other boats and we had called out to her but we really just wanted to give her a big hug. We all knew this was a harder day for her than anyone, so we were anxious to be with her. We eventually made it to the dock and it was a great feeling to switch off the engine for the last time. We all got off and met Mum, she was over the moon to see us back home and gave each of us a big hug and kiss. I couldn't really believe it, we were home.

Epilogue

Home was very different. The biggest changes were in the family – obviously Dad wasn't around and it took us some time to get used to the fact that he wouldn't be coming in the door. As I have said, being away, we hadn't really had to face into normal daily life with him not there.

Simon was of course a TD and within a week of getting home he had us out canvassing for the local elections. He was very focused and doing really well, it seemed that he had found something that he very much enjoyed. I was jealous of him to a degree not because I wanted to be a politician or anything but just that I would have loved to have been so sure of where I wanted to go and what I wanted to do. Simon was lucky which is a rare thing when people really like their job and look forward to their work.

Patrick and Emma were getting married and were heading off to Atlanta after the wedding for a couple of years. It was very exciting for them to have a whole new start once they were married. While Patrick lived in London for the previous few years he had been home often and I was going to miss him around the place.

Mum did her exams shortly after we got home and it was a strange role reversal to see her studying so hard. It must have been distracting for her to have us coming back only a week before her first exam. She really loved going to college and she is one of those infuriating mature students who reads all the books on the reading list, never misses lectures and always has her assignments in on time. Maybe that is the way all students should be. It was a great relief and delight for her to have us all home – like I said on the dock the day we arrived home, I am very lucky to have such a great mother.

Most of my friends were doing completely different things from when I had left. Many had moved to Dublin and were working in completely different areas. But I was relieved that most of them had remained basically the same.

Andrew, Tony and Rebecca each in their own way busied themselves with getting on with their respective careers. Within a few weeks of being home Andy was working for an engineering firm, Tony was working in a bar and Rebecca was off in Italy working as an au pair. They were all going back to college in October and were very much looking forward to it, while at the same time a little nervous. College life was going to be very different, and having been away for two years, even a little frightening.

Actually living in a house again was a challenge in itself for the four of us. We had so much space to move around in and a real bed was a luxury. Small things were also strange. We could run the tap without fear of running out of water, we could go for a walk when we wanted and we could drive a car again.

I think when, as a family, we look back at the years of 1998 and 1999 we will see them as a watershed. So much changed over this time that nothing really could ever be the same again. I suppose change is something that everyone fears, and for us it was strange because we had to confront it all at once.

During this voyage we encountered people from all walks of life, cultures and continents, from the little women who picked the tea leaves on the hills of Sri Lanka to the investment bankers of Singapore, from the musical guitar playing Fijians to the brash North Queenslanders, from the tiny Thai men to the giant Tongan women, from the fiery Egyptians to the humble Panamanian Indians, everywhere we went so much was different and so new to us that often we were simply amazed that this life – so different from Ireland – exists. As the journey pro-

gressed we quickly learned that while these places are in many ways so unlike here it is the similarities that are more striking. No matter where one happens to be born the fundamentals of human existence are the same and are merely approached from a different viewpoint or angle and set in a different environment. In Tonga for example the sense of community is much the same as rural Ireland, each Sunday religious service is a place not only of worship but also a social centre where everybody dresses in their best clothes. Believe me the giant Tongan women in their equally giant pink frilly dresses and the Tongan men in their woven palm leaf skirts are a sight to behold. When we visited the small village of Somosomo on a tiny island in Fiji and were invited into the corrugated iron home of a young couple who gave us tea and were so proud of their new-born daughter we could feel that these people are happy and content with what they have.

Belarus is different. This is a part of the world where laughs are rare and hope is even scarcer and where the burden of daily life has all but broken an amazingly proud people. Sail Chernobyl was a long voyage with a collection of stories and challenges, some difficult and very sad, some fantastic and full of laughs. It has I hope made a difference. We are proud that we have managed, even if only in a small way, to help a charity that has worked tirelessly to bring hope to this so often forgotten place – so much more needs to be done.

For the crew of *Golden Apple*, it has been an experience of a lifetime, a kaleidoscope of emotions. For me, well in writing this I have in many ways gone around the world twice, in my head at least, so to be honest I will probably stay away from the sea for a while. I will never forget what was sad or upsetting, and will always cherish those things that were beautiful and made me laugh over these two years. Have I changed? I don't know really, I suppose I must have but that's not really for me

to say. I do know I am looking forward to the future but on rainy days when all seems a little dull, I will be lucky enough to have the memory of that beautiful night arriving in the Galapagos – that was so perfect.

Appendix

Drawing of Golden Apple

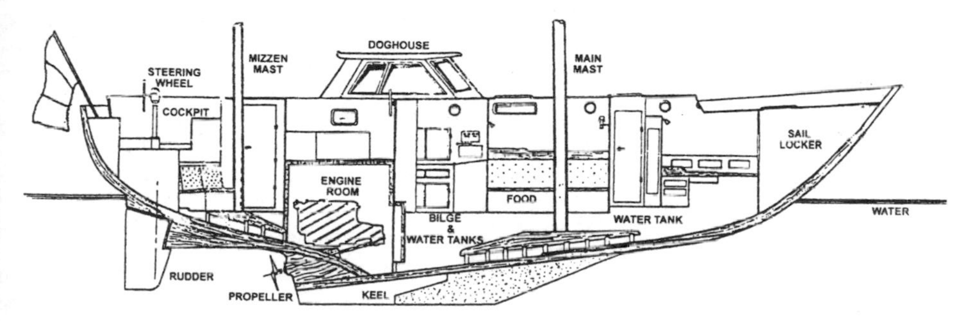

GOLDEN APPLE

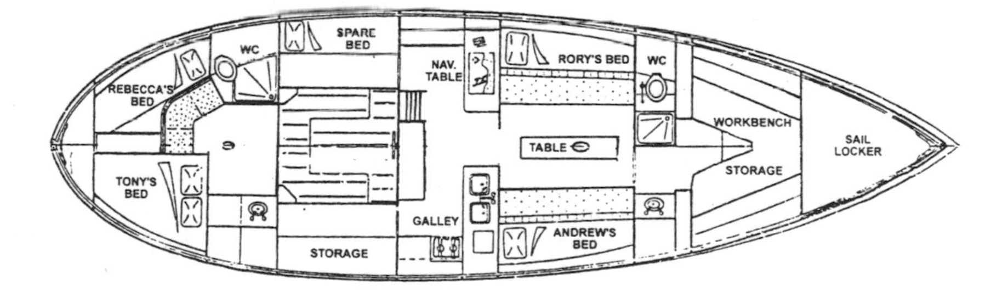